LIBERTY DENIED

DONNA A. DEMAC

LIBERTY DENIED

The Current Rise
of Censorship in America

Preface by ARTHUR MILLER

Introduction by LARRY McMURTRY

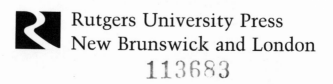

Rutgers University Press
New Brunswick and London

Library of Congress Cataloging-in-Publication Data

Demac, Donna A.
Liberty denied

Includes index.
1. Censorship—United States.   2. Freedom of the press—
United States.   3. Freedom of speech—United States.
4. Freedom of information—United States.   5. Official
secrets—United States.   I. Title.
Z658.U5D45   1988   363.3'1   88-17941
ISBN 0-8135-1544-0 (cloth)
ISBN 0-8135-1545-9 (pbk.)

CONTENTS

Author's Acknowledgments

My appreciation is due to the PEN American Center Freedom-to-Write Committee for inviting me to take on this project. PEN executive director Karen Kennerly, Walter Karp, and Martha Lear gave pivotal support, always with a deft, light-handed touch. I want especially to thank Sara Blackburn for her invaluable editorial guidance. Rochelle Lefkowitz, Edythea Ginis Selman, and Marlie Wasserman helped ensure that the book would reach a wider audience than do many works of a similar nature.

Gary Bass, Anne-Marie Buitrago, David Cole, Martin Garbus, Harry Hammitt, Ann Heanue, Bernadine Hoduski, Leanne Katz, Nancy Kranich, Quin Shea, and Gary Stern responded to my requests for information generously and with admirable speed. Doug Cordell was my able, resourceful research assistant, helped in the latter stages by Patrice Silverstein.

Philip Mattera critiqued and made valuable suggestions for each chapter. He and our son, Thomas, who arrived not long ago, enhanced this project in the most important, daily sorts of ways.

PEN American Center

International P.E.N. is an association of poets, playwrights, essayists, editors, novelists, and translators. It was founded in 1921 in London, and many of its eighty-six centers (located in sixty-five countries around the world), including the American Center, date back to the early 1920s. PEN's initial mandate and continuing purpose is to foster an international collegiality among writers so that we may learn about the literature of other cultures directly from those who are making it, and to protect the freedom of the writer and of all forms of expression wherever and whenever endangered.

Toward this second goal, the Freedom-to-Write Committee of PEN American Center works on behalf of approximately seventy-five writers and issues of censorship in about thirty countries each year. Since 1980, the Committee has become increasingly concerned with First Amendment violations and other forms of censorship in the United States: Book bannings in school libraries, the pernicious restrictions imposed on foreign travelers under the ideological provisions of the 1952 Immigration Act, misuse of libel laws, and government jamming of the Freedom of Information Act are but some of the issues PEN has taken up. As the number of incidents grew (and our status as the freest country in the world could no longer be assumed), the Committee believed it important to present them together—to be read, interpreted, and understood in the single context of the right to free expression and information we, as Americans, expect to hold.

PEN American Center wishes to thank Donna Demac for her exhaustive research and lucid presentation of material at once complex and confoundingly simple; Freedom-to-Write Committee member Walter Karp for his elegant overview that leads us into the study; former International P.E.N. President Arthur Miller for his preface that locates the report for all of us through one writer's experience. Our appreciation goes also to American PEN President Susan Sontag and Freedom-to-Write Co-Chair Faith Sale for their wisdom and guidance from initial research to publication; to Walter Karp, as well as Carol Ascher and Martha Lear, for their work in initiating the project; to Sara Blackburn for her deft and sensitive editing; and to Freedom-to-Write staff Helen Graves and Andrea Gambino for their quick and intelligent solutions to any problems that arose. Many others have devoted much time and thought to the publication of this book: Jules Feiffer, who donated the cover art, and Louise Fili, who donated the cover design; Lawrence Kramer, for his equally heroic work in the design and desktop publishing of the book, and Peter Wentzel of Kramer Communications, for careful typing under tough deadlines. Rochelle Lefkowitz and the staff of Pro-Media conceived and executed the entire publicity campaign, without which *Liberty Denied* could not reach the audience for which it was written.

The writing and publication of *Liberty Denied* were made possible by the generous support of the Deer Creek Foundation, the Field Foundation, and the J. Roderick MacArthur Foundation. We are particularly indebted to Richard Boone of the Field Foundation, who extended invaluable advice and direction at every stage of the project.

Finally, we wish to bring to the reader's attention other organizations that work to protect free expression and that have greatly assisted PEN's efforts over the years: the Committee to Protect Journalists, the Fund for Free Expression, the National Coalition Against Censorship, the American Library Association's Intellectual Freedom Committee, the American Civil Liberties Union, People for the American Way, Index on Censorship, and Article 19. Article 19, founded two years ago in London, will publish *Handbook on Freedom of Information and Censorship*—a worldwide analysis and survey—in the United States in September 1988.

Karen Kennerly
Executive Director

International P.E.N. Charter

International P.E.N. affirms that:

Literature, national though it be in origin, knows no frontiers, and should remain common currency between nations in spite of political or international upheavals.

In all circumstances, and particularly in time of war, works of art and libraries, the patrimony of humanity at large, should be left untouched by national or political passion.

Members of the PEN should at all times use what influence they have in favor of good understanding and mutual respect between nations; they pledge themselves to do their utmost to dispel race, class and national hatreds and to champion the ideal of one humanity living in peace in one world.

The PEN stands for the principle of unhampered transmission of thought within each nation and between all nations, and members pledge themselves to oppose any form of suppression of freedom of expression in the country and community to which they belong.

The PEN declares for a free press and opposes arbitrary censorship in time of peace. It believes that the necessary advance of the world towards a more highly organized political and economic order renders a free criticism of governments, administrations and institutions imperative. And since freedom implies voluntary restraint, members pledge themselves to oppose such evils of a free press and mendacious publication, deliberate falsehood, and distortion of facts for political and personal ends.

Preface to 1988 Edition

I am really the last person in the world who ought to be making an unmitigated defense of the media. Over several decades I have from time to time read things about myself ranging from thoughtless lies to savage portrayals that picture me as everything from a terrorist and communist traitor to an anti-Semite, plagiarist, and pimp, and not only by low-grade anonymous newspaper people and gossip columnists but also by heavy critics and even one or two book authors of most exquisite literary reputation and wide influence. Recently even my face has been described as sinister—and in a "liberal" magazine. I was twice on the verge of starting suits for libel but in the end persuaded myself to desist. My reasons were practical but also matters of principle.

Practically, a suit would simply spread untruths about me even further and publicize the vaporings of their authors even more than they had been, but even more important, suing a writer seemed to cross a principle that I respect and cherish more than even my own reputation: the freedom to speak and print—yes, even to speak lies and print them. It cannot be right to defend liberty by limiting its use, even by those who really care little about it.

This isn't to say that truth will out in the long run, unless millennia is what you mean by the long run. For example, if I. F. Stone's thesis about Socrates is sound, it has taken better than two thousand years to correct the impression that he was a liberal condemned by reactionaries to die for the principle of truth-telling candor in the teaching of the young. Instead, he may have been a conservative so bitterly opposed to democracy that he literally chose to get himself killed in order to defame it. Similarly, there have been a number of recent studies to show that the horrible Pharisees were in fact liberals of the age of whom Jesus was actually one, but whose repute had to be besmirched by later writers whose purpose was to separate Jesus from his real—but too radical—supporters.

Whether private persons or government feels offended, the problem is the same, namely, how to prevent those who would write nasty or discomfiting things from doing so. The quickest cure is one or another form of censorship, but as this study shows, the consequences for the very fabric of a society are grave and at the present time are not at all settled in either liberal or responsible conservative opinion. This book surveys the realities of American options in a concise and nonpartisan fashion, and tellingly demonstrates what book banning, official secrecy, and other forms of censorship imply for our liberties and our future as a free society—or more accurately, a society still struggling to define what freedom entails.

Arthur Miller

Introduction to 1990 Edition

By chance I was thumbing through William James's classic *Varieties of Religious Experience* just before I picked up *Liberty Denied*, and the thought occurred that the latter might just as aptly be called *Varieties of American Censorship.*

That hoary truism, "All politics is local," might serve as an appropriate subtext for Donna Demac's able and thorough study. All censorship might be seen as local, too, particularly if you consider such things as government bureaus, regulatory agencies, cabinets, councils, courtrooms, departments, divisions, and the thousand other official purlieus of our bustling democracy to be localities of a sort.

Read from that perspective, this book is a kind of geography of American censorship, a medical atlas if you will, showing in detail how censorship's tumorous cells are distributed in clusters throughout the body politic.

Among the several morals this book points is that good citizenship takes energy. We are in the main an open society and a great deal of information about the workings of the government can be had by those who are determined to get it. In most instances the information is not absolutely hidden; it is, however, cleverly sequestered, concealed behind a thicket of daunting forms and complex routes of access. The hope of censors within officialdom is that few will make it through the thicket, or complete the route.

In the end, though, it may be the offical and to some degree high-profile cells of censorship that can be defeated, if only because there are people and organizations who know where to find these cells, and who have the energy, persistence, and commitment necessary to defeat them. PEN is one such organization, the ACLU is another, and there are many more.

But there are localities (in the literal sense) where the Stealth bombers of censorship operate so quietly and at such low altitudes that the radar of the anti-censorship forces can only occasionally detect them. School boards might pressure a teacher to remove from a course-list a book because one parent has objected. My novel *Texasville* was thus removed from a class reading list at a high school in Texas.

Local libraries come frequently under the threat; there is scarcely a library in America that doesn't contain books the fundamentalist mentality will disapprove of. *Liberty Denied* cites many cases of the sort of local censorship that is difficult to monitor in a comprehensive way.

Reading this book convinces me once again that censorship is almost always rooted in fear, and the fears that promote and propel it run a gamut from terrible to silly. Some of the most terrible censorings stem from the fear of the loss of political power or control, but a great many others have more trivial origins. Parents read a book and decide their child shouldn't, on the grounds that the book will make the child a bad person, a godless person, a sexually promiscuous person, or, at the very least, a person the parents will no longer like.

Similarly, but at a higher altitude, a president reads an intelligence finding and decides that if the nation were really permitted to know what was going on the nation might become bad, godless, unruly, or, at the very least, a nation he wouldn't approve of.

So the book or the finding gets squelched, kept from the child or from us in the name of some vision of order and appropriateness to which few children and even fewer nations can every really conform.

What is feared, in the end, is the power of the word, or the word's extensions and emissaries. It is fear of this same power that has led so many dictators to send some of the best of those emissaries—leading citizens of the dominion of the word —to the stake, the block, or the gulag.

It is up to us all who value freedom of expression as the high and indivisible right that it is to put some energy into our vigilance so that we can detect the Stealth bombers of the censors, however low or locally they fly.

This book will help in our plane-spotting. It reminds us, too, that the freedoms we value most won't come in the mail. They require something of us: a level of attention; a striving.

Larry McMurtry

1

"LIBERTY'S NATION"

The Foundations of Free Expression in the United States

Censorship. For most Americans the word brings to mind newspaper editors being jailed, publications appearing only after sensitive passages have been removed, government officials screening news scripts before they are read on the air, opponents of official policy ending up in a gulag. In short, the word evokes the trappings of a police state.

For Americans, censorship usually is associated with troubling suppression that happens somewhere else. Soviets and Eastern Europeans are censored; foreign journalists in South Africa are censored; Chilean dissidents are censored.

Many of us believe that the United States is virtually free of such restrictions. People proudly point to the Bill of Rights as an impenetrable shield and boast that we Americans enjoy a kind of free speech that is almost absolute. Even when it is acknowledged that we are confronted with some limitations on expression, the admission is usually accompanied by the claim that such restrictions are much less severe than they are elsewhere in the world.

The reality of individual liberties in the United States is far more ambiguous. Although Walt Whitman described America as "Liberty's nation," the history of freedom of expression in this country has been a complex mixture of a commitment to personal rights—undeniably greater than in most other countries—and a marked intolerance of dissident and unorthodox views. The extent to which the ideals of liberty have been

1

realized has been determined by a continual tug-of-war between government tendencies to suppress those deemed subversive, and citizen initiatives aimed at expanding the sphere of freedom.

Ironically, during the same period in which the United States has been celebrating the bicentennial of the Constitution, freedom of expression is in a very precarious state. Repressive government policies and campaigns by conservative social groups have severely narrowed the range of public discourse and have thrown a cloak of fear and secrecy across the country. Such values as openness, diversity, and tolerance have been pushed aside in favor of conformity, patriotism, and national security. Among the signs of the times:

- Leading newspapers are harassed and threatened with criminal prosecution by high-level federal officials for publishing sensitive information.

- The FBI, acting under a presidential order, conducts a massive program of surveillance against groups protesting the administration's policies in Central America.

- Hundreds of thousands of federal officials and employees of government contractors are forced to sign secrecy agreements that subject them to criminal sanctions.

- Right-wing groups coerce public school officials across the country into denying students access to "dangerous" books, ranging from Chaucer's *Canterbury Tales* to the novels of Kurt Vonnegut.

- Self-appointed guardians of morality record the license-plate numbers of people entering X-rated movie theaters and report the information to the police.

- The Supreme Court rules that school principals have broad authority to censor the content of student newspapers.

Much of the responsibility for this climate rests with the Reagan and Bush administrations, which have insulated government activities as though the country were under siege. Power has been centralized in the White House to an extent not seen before now in peacetime. A rigid preoccupation with national security and terrorism has produced sweeping restrictions on the amount and quality of information available to the public—and even to Congress. The new standards of secrecy have also been extended to broad categories of academic and scientific research. Commercial database providers have been pressured to deny their services to certain customers.

The White House has also given encouragement to those outside government who pursue their own repressive agendas. As a result of their efforts, individual freedom has been jeopardized in classrooms, workplaces, theaters, and libraries. The new victims of censorship are both young and old. Tens of thousands of children have been denied access to rich works of literature, history, and scientific thought. Following the lead of the attorney general and other government officials, self-appointed antivice squads have sought to punish people for the possession of sexually explicit material.

The consequences of these campaigns are grave. Not only do they divide people against one another, but they often intimidate individuals to the point that censorship becomes self-induced. It is difficult to act according to one's beliefs in an atmosphere of constant disapproval, and sometimes conformity offers relief from the pain of peer pressure. But once people mute their own voices, the censors have achieved their ultimate victory. As Walt Whitman wrote: "There is no week nor day nor hour, when tyranny may not enter upon this country, if the people lose their supreme confidence in themselves—and lose their roughness and spirit of defiance."

Attorney Floyd Abrams, a specialist in freedom of expression, has stated that the Reagan administration "trumped" the First Amendment, meaning that whatever it chose to do on the pretext of national security took precedence over competing constitutional considerations. It is true as well that the American people have often trumped their own liberty, accepting official rationales that violated their rights.

This lack of skepticism, which reached epidemic proportions during the early years of the Reagan administration, is dangerous for a democratic society. No government holds itself accountable, and few, if any, favor scrutiny, much less dissent. The public's failure to remain vigilant during a period as fraught with censorship as the 1980s amounts to a gullibility crisis of major proportions.

One explanation for Americans' unwarranted tolerance of government misconduct is a lack of historical understanding. Evaluating the significance of actions in the present is especially difficult for a society that approaches each day in isolation from its past. We Americans toss out traces of yesterday as quickly as our buildings are torn down in neighborhoods slated for redevelopment.

Today's attitudes toward freedom of speech cannot be separated from the past. A look back to the earlier debates and struggles over dissent, pornography, book banning, and other areas of expression helps inform our understanding of the climate today.

Historically, a ban on prior restraint was considered the essence of freedom of expression. The British legal commentator Sir William Blackstone wrote: "Every free man has an undoubted right to lay what sentiments he pleases before the public; to forbid this is to destroy freedom of the press; but if he publishes what is improper, mischievous, or illegal, he must take the consequences."

Despite this axiom, prior restraint was a central feature of government censorship during the colonial era. British law made criticism of an official a criminal offense—"seditious libel." Nevertheless, many people were outspoken, and printers were frequently prosecuted. James Franklin, the older brother of Benjamin, was thrown into jail on several occasions for criticizing colonial officials.

The first crack in the all-powerful state came in 1735, when a jury hearing the prosecution of publisher John Peter Zenger for seditious libel rejected the judge's instructions and delivered a verdict of innocence on the grounds that truth should be recognized as a defense.

Even after the country became independent and the Constitution with its Bill of Rights was adopted, great confusion still prevailed as to the extent of individual freedom of expression. The first major test of the First Amendment came with the Sedition Act of 1798. This law, which provided jail penalties and severe fines for criticism of the president and other members of the government, was used by the Federalist administration of John Adams to suppress its Republican opponents. The enactment of the law was part of a campaign to centralize the

4

government, muzzle the press, and move toward a one-party state.

The statute did not have its intended effect. Rather than be intimidated, opponents of the heavy-handed measures of the Federalists became more outspoken than ever. Many courageous editors risked imprisonment, and many publications were seized by government soldiers. In fact, the debates generated by this confrontation helped define what the First Amendment—which had been adopted with little discussion—meant in a democratic society.

The issue was put most clearly by George Hay, a member of the Virginia House of Delegates. Hay argued that if the First Amendment had any meaning, it had to be understood as preventing the government from punishing *any* speech; otherwise it would be a mere privilege rather than a right. As for the press, Hay insisted that it must be protected by "a total exemption from any law making any publication whatever criminal."

Hay's view represented an ideal that the country has moved toward. But our progress has frequently been impeded by the conflicting impulses of those who hold political and economic power and are thus fearful of challenges to the status quo.

In certain areas that fall outside the province of criticizing the state—such as potential libel and sexually explicit expression—laws against censorship have been strengthened considerably at both state and federal levels during this century. In such major conflicts as the movement for civil rights and the creationism debate, the First Amendment has been recognized as the cornerstone of all other freedoms. One of the most famous instances came in the early 1960s. As the civil rights movement spread throughout the South, state authorities tried to bar national press coverage by implementing libel laws that exacted stiff penalties for damage to a person's reputation. The Supreme Court, refusing to permit libel law to be used as a shield for racism, established a new rule that required public officials who sued the press to demonstrate that the defendants had shown reckless disregard of the truth.

Unfortunately, the Court has not expanded protection for political dissent. Although it ruled in the Pentagon Papers case in 1971 that the government could not restrict access to public information without proof that this would endanger national security, subsequent Court decisions have diminished this victory by articulating broad new powers of the state to withhold documents and to restrict individual expression. Some of these decisions upheld the use of secrecy contracts requiring government employees to submit their independent writings and speeches for prior government review. In this way, the long-standing prohibition against prior restraint has been partially reversed, and our nation has taken a giant step closer to the strictures that prevail in Britain, where large categories of information are banned from publication under an Official Secrets Act.

During the Cold War of the 1950s, the American public became accustomed to broadly stated claims of national security that were rationalized by the alleged peril posed by communism. Government secrecy became institutionalized in such areas as atomic energy; dissidents were subjected to surveillance and harassment; and elaborate covert intelligence networks were set up to operate abroad and at home. These practices continued for decades, and they were given a special place in the policies of the Reagan administration.

Now that we are seeing a lessening of tensions between the superpowers, the question arises as to whether the new atmosphere will lead to a reduction in the repressive apparatus of government. In the Soviet Union, there are encouraging indications of a broadening of individual rights, although it is not possible to predict their durability. But where are the signs of *glasnost* in America? The United States is at a turning point with regard to freedom of expression. The alternatives are clear: We can choose to remain indifferent about the erosion of our rights. In that case the Reagan era's legacy of fear and ignorance will extend into the 1990s, and the country will continue on the slide toward unchecked government power. Or, like our predecessors in 1798, we can challenge those who have qualified and curtailed our freedoms and begin an examination of censorship American-style in order to transform our muted voices into calls for liberty.

2
BANNED IN THE USA

Censorship in America's Schools and Libraries

Our children's imaginations have to be bounded.
—Vicki Frost, parent in court suit to have certain books removed from Church Hill, Tennessee, public schools[1]

Controversy over access to ideas and information has permeated America's institutions of learning at all levels in recent years. Various books, films, classroom exercises, and student publications have been removed, banned, and even burned by parents and others who have considered them dangerous. Freedom of inquiry, as well as student rights of speech and expression, have increasingly been put in jeopardy. These assaults, which emerge in different parts of the country but are often orchestrated by national organizations, have cast a shadow of censorship over the nation's classrooms.

Tradition versus Tolerance

Since its origin in the nineteenth century, American public school education has had as one of its primary goals the assimilation of diverse peoples and the teaching of social tolerance. Yet these democratic values always have been in conflict with the wish of many parents to have their children exposed only to particular religious and moral views. In the early twentieth century, the increasingly secular nature of public education was followed by a backlash of protest by such parents and their allies. One result was the attempt by some states to outlaw the teaching of evolution in favor of the biblical version of creation. In 1925 the issues were fought out in the famous Scopes trial in Dayton, Tennessee. In a courtroom drama that drew national attention, John Scopes, a schoolteacher, failed in his challenge to a new state law that forbade the teaching of evolution in the public schools. Similar laws already had been passed in Oklahoma and Mississippi and had been introduced in half of all state legislatures.

Public education survived these challenges, but with the exception of particular schools and particular teachers, after World War II classroom instruction became increasingly standardized and increasingly bland in content. As Frances FitzGerald wrote in *America Revised*: "The histories of the fifties were implacable, seamless. Inside their covers America was perfect, the greatest nation in the world, and the embodiment of democracy, freedom and technological progress."[2]

This complacent self-image of America did not last for long. The social tensions that had been brewing within American society began to rise to the surface, and schools, like other institutions, were forced to adapt. In 1954 the Supreme Court called for the elimination of racial segregation in education "with all deliberate speed." A decade later, in 1963, the Court affirmed the secular nature of state-sponsored education in a ruling that banned the recitation of prayers in public schools. These two landmark cases helped pave the way for a transformation of public education in the 1960s.

That transformation was a key element of the Johnson administration's "Great Society" programs, which pumped massive quantities of federal money into schools. The Elementary and Secondary Education Act and Project Head Start, both enacted in 1965, were explicitly intended to improve opportunities for groups—including the disabled and racial and ethnic minorities—that had been shortchanged by local educational systems.

During this period, major philanthropic institutions, especially the Ford and Carnegie foundations, also spent heavily on education. Much of their emphasis was on modifying curricula and textbooks to portray more accurately the diversity of American society. Grants were used to commission texts that showed black and Asian faces as well as white ones; that depicted women as holding paying jobs; that recounted a history in which the United States was not always the knight in shining armor. Reading lists were expanded to include novels that portrayed young people as having doubts about their lives and sometimes going astray. Educators were encouraged to design classroom materials that prodded students to ask themselves questions about their personal views, their families, and society—in other words, to take a more critical approach to the world.

The Mounting Challenge

Some parents regarded these changes with alarm, and they were encouraged in their resistance by conservative political and cultural organizations that viewed the expanded curricula as offensive meddling by the federal government and the eastern liberal establishment. These criticisms of the innovations in public education were part of the general dismay traditionalists were expressing at other changes in the values of many young people. The rise of a counterculture, the interest in Eastern religions, political radicalism, and myriad other such character-istics of youth in the 1960s were regarded as dangerous chal-lenges to authority and scandalized large segments of those devoted to traditional moral and religious values. Although many aspects of this social upheaval turned out to be short-lived, the traditionalists who believed that their own values were under siege launched a crusade against what they branded "secular humanism."

One of the earliest and most hated targets was a new fifth- and sixth-grade social science curriculum introduced in 1970. Funded by the National Science Foundation, "Man: A Course of Study" (MACOS) used the examination of animal behavior to raise questions about human motivation. It emphasized open-ended discussion and independent thinking. Adopted in forty-seven states by 1974, the new course assumed that teachers and students accepted evolution as the process by which human development had come about. This assumption made it the center of so much controversy around the country that by 1982 the National Science Foundation ended its involvement in the reform of science curricula.[3]

The critics sometimes took their battle into the streets. In 1974 citizens in Kanawha County, West Virginia, outraged by the use of what they called "dirty" and "antireligious" textbooks, launched a campaign that included the fire-bombings of school buildings and protest strikes by coal miners. Eight thousand children were kept home from school; picketers closed bus depots and grocery stores; several people were shot. After months of upheaval, the protesters gained significant concessions. The county board of education adopted new textbook selection guidelines that excluded many of the disputed volumes and set up screening committees of laymen to review books for sensitive content.

While most textbook critics did not adopt the tactics of the righteous rioters of West Virginia, the traditionalist movement grew apace. By 1981, according to a study done by the Association of American Publishers and the American Library Association, incidents of censorship were widespread and rising at a frightening rate.[4]

The Dirty Dozen

The range of objectionable material cited by the textbook crusaders is vast.[5] Aside from their insistence that the biblical story of creation be granted at least equal status with evolution in describing the origins of human life, they have been militant about any text that reflects the social transformations of the past thirty years. The movements for civil rights, women's liberation, and disarmament are all suspect. Anything that veers from traditional perspectives on sexuality, social roles, parental authority, and a wide variety of other such matters is considered taboo. Sometimes a whole text is considered objectionable; in other cases only particular passages are specified as offensive. "Dangerous" words and phrases have been found in dictionaries, nursery rhymes, the works of Shakespeare, and home economics texts. One group in Tennessee pressured teachers to remove from their classrooms Halloween pictures of witches and ghosts, as well as the Easter bunny, on the grounds that they introduced counterreligious elements to their children's education.[6]

According to a survey by Dr. Lee Burress of the University of Wisconsin,[7] the titles that have been the most frequently challenged are

1. *The Catcher in the Rye* by J. D. Salinger
2. *The Grapes of Wrath* by John Steinbeck
3. *Of Mice and Men* by John Steinbeck
4. *Go Ask Alice* (anonymous)
5. *Forever. . .* by Judy Blume

6. *Our Bodies, Ourselves* by the Boston Women's Health Collective
7. *The Adventures of Huckleberry Finn* by Mark Twain
8. *The Learning Tree* by Gordon Parks
9. *My Darling, My Hamburger* by Paul Zindel
10. *1984* by George Orwell
11. *Black Boy* by Richard Wright
12. *The Canterbury Tales* by Geoffrey Chaucer

While most of these are works of fiction, the protesters have also been offended by straightforward reportage. In 1981 the board of education in Baileyville, Maine, decided to remove a book about the Vietnam War from the public school library. Written by a doctor who had treated seriously injured soldiers in Vietnam, *365 Days* was an attempt to inform people about the human costs of the war.[8] But many Baileyville residents were offended by the book's realism, and by the inclusion of certain four-letter words.[9]

The power of parents to veto the selection of books by teachers and libraries has become a hotly debated issue in our time. The opposition to *365 Days* was based partly in an attempt by local parents to shield their children from an explosive period in American history. It was also a rejection of a pedagogical approach in which young people are exposed to a wide range of ideas and information.

The advocates of narrow exposure have made use of a 1978 law, commonly referred to as the Hatch Amendment, that requires parental consent before students undergo psychological testing. Technically, the legislation applies only to federally funded programs, but many groups have used it to legitimize attacks on programs and curricula that are neither psychological in focus nor funded by Washington. Instead they have argued that the law supports the removal of books, courses, and teaching methods that challenge students to think independently.

A group of parents in Westmoreland County, Pennsylvania, has invoked the Hatch Amendment in a suit against the public schools over use of the textbook *Adolescents Today*, claiming that the book promotes "secular humanism" and condones contraception instead of endorsing abstinence from sexual activity. In Missouri the requirement that students read John Steinbeck's *Of Mice and Men* was attacked as a violation of the

Hatch Amendment; in Texas, Stephen King's novel *Cujo* was denounced on the same grounds.

In 1984 U.S. Department of Education regulations broadened the scope of the Hatch Amendment, making it applicable to classroom questions about political points of view, personal behavior, and students' attitudes and feelings. Despite widespread opposition and a disclaimer by the law's sponsor, Senator Orrin Hatch, the Education Department has not rescinded these regulations. Such cues from the federal government have nationwide impact, and numerous states have passed Hatch Amendment clones that prohibit various kinds of classroom instruction. A Michigan law, for example, forbids teachers from providing information on abortion.

Challenges against books, particularly challenges that invoke the Hatch Amendment, have frequently succeeded in transforming attempts at censorship into battles over control. Parents, asserting their rights under the banner of local control, are pitted against school officials, teachers, and librarians asserting their traditional authority over public education. The parents have found allies in conservative groups such as Phyllis Schlafly's Eagle Forum, Pat Robertson's Freedom Council, and the National Association of Christian Educators. Teachers and administrators opposed to book banning have turned to the Intellectual Freedom Committee of the American Library Association, the National Coalition Against Censorship, People for the American Way, and the National Education Association.

Sometimes the two sides have reached compromises on book selection procedures. But the fact that the parents may well have what they consider good intentions is outweighed by the reality that what they are doing is inimical to free expression and good education. Kurt Vonnegut, whose books have literally been burned by local activists (and whose *Slaughterhouse-Five* is number 13 on the list above), puts the matter bluntly: "Can the Constitution of the United States be made a scrap of paper by appeals to what sincere persons believe the laws of God and nature to be?"[10]

The Danger of "Dumbing Down"

Textbook selection policies vary across the country. Roughly half the states exercise state-level control over the range of choices, which means that local school districts are barred from using state funds to buy books that are not on the approved list. In other areas, books are chosen through a local review process that may include a board comprised of teachers, parents, and administrators. A handful of large states are of special importance because they account for a major share of the national textbook market and are therefore accorded special attention by textbook critics and publishers.

For many years Texas has been a primary target of the organized textbook censors. Two activists in particular, Mel and Norma Gabler, have made a career of preparing lists of books that, they charge, foster "the religion of secular humanism," "one-worldism," sexual promiscuity, and other such behavior. Widely regarded as successful practitioners of grass-roots lobbying, the Gablers have assisted hundreds of book-banning campaigns throughout the country. Their efforts have received support from organizations like the Heritage Foundation that seek to limit government influence on education.

The Gablers' greatest success in their own state came in 1974, when the Texas legislature passed a law requiring textbooks to identify evolution as only one of several explanations of humankind's origin. The couple's influence in Texas was virtually inviolate for the following decade. Each year the state textbook committee held a hearing at which complainants—and only complainants—could testify about proposed texts. In the face of this pressure, publishers have often agreed to modify their texts to make them acceptable. For example, in a biology text approved for the 1981 school year, the word "evolution" did not appear anywhere. Publishers say that given the large sums of money at stake, they have little choice but to engage in a process that has come to be known as the "dumbing down" of texts. As a consequence of this practice, a sizable portion of the latest generation of high school students in states like Texas have heard little mention of Darwin, evolution, and other "sensitive" topics.

The Gablers have been challenged in recent years thanks to campaigns mounted by local citizens and assisted by national anticensorship organizations such as People for the American Way. This activism helped bring about a 1984 ruling by the Texas attorney general that set aside the policy on evolution as an unconstitutional intrusion of religion into state matters. The contents of biology and other textbooks have since been revised, though the problem of "dumbing down" is still with us.

While it is heartening that book-banning crusaders like the Gablers are being challenged more effectively, they clearly have had a lasting and negative effect on the quality of American education. Countless educators have been forced to divert huge amounts of time and energy from teaching to defending their curricula. And Paul Putnam of the National Education Association points out that even when the censors lose or even when a particular book-banning campaign has ended, educators may still be inclined to engage in self-censorship to avoid trouble. A teacher may decide not to use materials that have elicited complaints elsewhere; a librarian may decide not to order a book that generated controversy in a nearby community. Every such act is a victory for the forces of closed-mindedness.

Religion in the Public Schools

Behind most of the textbook battles is the larger issue of what place religion should occupy in public education. In recent years conservatives have renewed their opposition to what they regard as the troubling absence of religion from the classroom. They have repeatedly called for school prayer, religious instruction, a greater general emphasis on religion in subjects such as social studies, and the teaching of the biblical story of creation. They continue to denounce "secular humanism."

Some religious zealots actually would like to eliminate public education entirely. Jerry Falwell has written:

> I hope I live to see the day when, as in the early days of our country, we won't have any public schools. The churches will have taken them over again and Christians will be running them. What a happy day that will be![11]

We have noted that local religious activists often receive support from national conservative organizations and fundamentalist bodies, yet the movement has also received some measure of assistance from mainstream religious denominations that share their concern about a decline in morality and the reliance on scientific explanations in curricula.[12]

In the name of religious principles, the forces of censorship have mounted some ambitious campaigns. A group of parents in Hawkins County, Tennessee, sued their school system for using

14

a Holt, Rinehart & Winston textbook series for grades 1 through 8. They charged that the series and other "anti-Christian" books taught disobedience to parents, "witchcraft," "one-worldism," and "secular humanism." By refusing to offer alternative texts, the parents alleged, the Hawkins County School System unconstitutionally violated the children's religious freedom. The case received support from Conservative Women for America and was argued by CWA's attorney, Michael Farris, formerly head of the Moral Majority organization in Washington State.

In the lower court, the parents' arguments were affirmed and students were allowed to opt out of regular course instruction to avoid exposure to the contested material, which included selections from *The Diary of Anne Frank, The Wizard of Oz,* and "Cinderella." The court also ordered the school board to reimburse some of the parents for the cost of sending their children to other schools while the case was being decided.

The decision was appealed, and the case eventually reached the U.S. Court of Appeals, which ruled in August 1987 that nothing in the Holt series required students to deny or affirm any religious beliefs:

> When asked to comment on a reading assignment, a student would be free to give the Biblical interpretation of the material or to interpret it from a different value base. The only conduct compelled by the defendants was reading and discussing the material in the Holt series, and hearing other students' interpretations of those materials. This is the exposure to which the plaintiffs objected.[13]

The appeals court properly found that while a student had a right to maintain his or her religious beliefs in the classroom, the same student has no right, in a public school, to be shielded from the possibly divergent views of others. [14]

A Revision of Tactics

Faced with such legal setbacks as the one in Hawkins County, the textbook censors have adopted a new approach. Instead of continuing to press for religious content in texts, they have sought to exploit the First Amendment for their own purposes by claiming that the books they found objectionable in effect promoted a "religion."

This clever approach was adopted in a suit brought by 624 plaintiffs who claimed that the entire curriculum of the Mobile, Alabama, public school system was unconstitutional because it taught "secular humanism"—which the plaintiffs claimed was a religion. Their line of reasoning was well received by Judge Brevard Hand, who in fact had encouraged the plaintiffs to bring the case after an earlier decision of his, which upheld school prayer, was struck down by the Supreme Court. Judge Hand's March 1987 ruling in the curriculum case prohibited use of more than forty social studies texts. The objectionable passages included:

> Just as you make mistakes, so do parents. They are only human. People of all races and cultural backgrounds should be shown as having high ideals and goals.
> What can stop the spread of cheating? The foundation of integrity has to come from within a person.

The plaintiffs' case was supported by the right-wing Rutherford Institute, whose director, John Whitehead, has called for an "ideological battle to determine who's going to win the schools." Indirect assistance also came from then Alabama governor George Wallace, who signed a consent decree in 1985 pledging to have "secular humanism" removed from state textbooks.

Judge Hand's decision was overturned by the U.S. Court of Appeals in August 1987.[15] The court sidestepped the issue of whether what the plaintiffs called "secular humanism" is a religion by concluding that in any event they had failed to prove that the use of the textbooks in question was a violation of the Establishment Clause of the First Amendment. The texts, the court found, contained ideas that were consistent with theistic religion as well as secular humanism, but it noted that "mere consistency with religious tenets is insufficient to constitute unconstitutional advancement of religion." The justices went on to find that the reason for the use of the particular texts "was purely secular," while the plaintiffs' case boiled down only to the complaint that "the historical treatment of religion in the challenged textbooks is inadequate."

The Supreme Court and the Religious Wars

The plague of censorship in schools and libraries originated in part with the reaction of the religious right to the 1963

Supreme Court decision prohibiting prayer in the public schools. Despite this ruling and many other defeats in the courts, the creationists have kept up their campaign to have the biblical version of the origin of the world taught in public schools. Having failed in their initial drive to have the theory of evolution banned from curricula, creationists have in recent years focused on getting equal time for the biblical view.

When this was rejected as a clear attempt to introduce religion into the classroom, fundamentalists came up with two alternative approaches. In addition to the attempt to challenge objectionable texts on the grounds that they advocated a religion of their own, they invented the notion of "creation science" in the hope that the term would allow their cause to skirt the First Amendment's restrictions on the recognition of religion—the Establishment Clause.

State legislatures in both Arkansas and Louisiana accepted the argument that creationism could be construed as a science that ought to be included in secular courses of study. Nevertheless, the legislation that each passed in order to give this supposed science equal time was struck down by federal judges. Louisiana appealed all the way to the Supreme Court, and the result was a June 1987 decision[16] that constituted the strongest blow yet to the creationist cause. The Court voted 7 to 2 to strike down the Louisiana law, which had forbidden the teaching of evolution unless instruction in the "science" of creationism was included as well. The Court decided that the law "violates the Establishment Clause of the First Amendment because it seeks to employ the symbolic and financial support of government to achieve a religious purpose." Stephen Jay Gould has written that as a result of the Court's decision the creationists' "legislative strategy, their linchpin ever since the Scopes trial, is kaput, at least for our generation." It would be consoling to believe that the creationists are in retreat, but their tenacity is well-known, and their withdrawal highly unlikely.

Censorship on Campus: Accuracy in Academia

Censorship of another sort emerged in American educational institutions in the 1980s. A new organization that called itself Accuracy in Academia set out to expose what it regarded as the liberal and Marxist bias of many professors in American universities. An offshoot of Reed Irvine's Accuracy in Media, AIA claimed to have "volunteer monitors" taping classroom lectures and keeping lists on two hundred campuses. In its newsletter, *Campus Report*, AIA listed names of specific professors and the nature of their purported offenses. Students across the country were encouraged to mount their own campaigns, prompting AIA supporters in Seattle to call a press conference to denounce the antinuclear bias they detected in the lectures of one local college professor.

Among others, Dr. Mark Reader of Arizona State University was attacked by AIA for spending "excessive" time in a political science course discussing the dangers of nuclear war. Saul Landau of the University of California at Davis found his class picketed on the day he planned to show a documentary about Cuba.[17]

The tactics of AIA—which was clearly concerned with ideology rather than accuracy— evoked opposition even among conservative groups, and the heyday of the organization was short. The practice of spying on campus was kept alive, however, by a group called Young America's Foundation, which has received funding from the U.S. Information Agency as well as from such supporters of the extreme right as Joseph Coors. Michael Boos, director of the foundation, boasted to a San Francisco TV reporter that his group has done more than any other to monitor left-wing activities on campus. Its own activities have included photographing activist students and faculty members, obtaining lists of people who have signed certain petitions, and keeping track of those who give speeches at rallies and write anti–Reagan administration articles in student newspapers. Boos also has claimed that the foundation provides campus intelligence to the FBI and the Justice Department.[18]

Censorship at Hazelwood High

"Student journalism is literally fighting for its life." This alarming statement by Mark Goodman, executive director of the Student Press Law Center, is based on events such as the one that took place at Hazelwood East High School in St. Louis in 1983. That May, the school's principal removed from a student publication two articles that he had found to be "too sensitive." One of the articles was about teen pregnancy; the other concerned the impact of divorce on children. Three students who worked on the newspaper sued, claiming that their First Amendment rights to write about controversial topics had been violated.

As this test case made its way to the Supreme Court, the predictions of its outcome were uncertain. Historically, decisions by school principals regarding student actions have been held by the courts to be sacrosanct. The judiciary has fostered a two-tier approach to the First Amendment, allowing school officials to censor pornographic and political speech by young people in a way that it did not find permissible for similar adult expression. In a 1969 exception, the Court ruled that prohibiting students from wearing armbands to protest the Vietnam War violated their free speech rights, thus establishing that students did have at least some independent First Amendment protection.[19] Yet as recently as 1986, it determined that high school officials could legally prohibit the use of "vulgar and offensive terms."[20]

Administrators have not been shy about using this power. Even as the Court was considering the Hazelwood case, two student editors of high school newspapers, one in Illinois and the other in Kentucky, were fired by their principals because of editorial disagreements. In Illinois, the editor had opposed the school board's student conduct code; in Kentucky, the editor— who was later reinstated— had printed an editorial calling for the return of pep rallies.

When the Court issued its ruling in the Hazelwood case in January 1988,[21] the majority argued that the power of school officials to oversee educational activities took precedence over the rights of students. Justice Byron White wrote for the majority:

> We hold that educators do not offend the First Amendment by exercising editorial control over the style and content of student speech in school-sponsored expressive activities so long as their actions are reasonably related to legitimate pedagogical concerns.

The problem, of course, is that the standard of "legitimate pedagogical concerns" can be used to justify the suppression of views that are embarrassing or distasteful to school officials. In his dissent, Justice William Brennan insisted that school sponsorship of a publication does not "license thought control in the high school." Brennan went on to state that granting blanket censorship authority to educators was hardly the way to teach children to respect the diversity of ideas that is fundamental to the American system.

The problem of censorship of student newspapers is not limited to high schools. College and university administrators have exhibited the same tendency to suppress what they consider embarrassing or improper writings. Ivan Holmes, who teaches journalism at the University of Arkansas, conducted a national survey of the situation in 1986 and determined that campus censorship is thriving. Summarizing his findings, Holmes wrote in the *Columbia Journalism Review:*

> Far too many university administrators are more concerned about their image than about the pursuit of truth. . . . On all 18 campuses I visited for this study someone was trying to intimidate the campus press in one way or another.[22]

The practice of censorship in the schools is a serious and troubling phenomenon. It is also a growing one. Across the nation, hundreds of grass-roots organizations are conducting broad-based attacks on school texts and library collections, while school administrators have been granted sweeping new powers to control student expression.

The recent Supreme Court ruling in the Hazelwood case has added momentum to the move away from free speech in the schools. Less than a month after the decision, courts in several states were already using it as the basis to uphold the censorship of student publications as well as the outright banning of books.

A federal judge in Jacksonville affirmed the right of Columbia County, Florida, school officials to remove certain texts—by Aristophanes and Chaucer—from the curriculum. The judge indicated that she agreed with the plaintiffs in the case, who had challenged the book banning as an infringement on the free speech rights of students, but said she was compelled by the Hazelwood case to rule in favor of the administrators. An appeals court in California cited *Hazelwood* in upholding the right of a high school principal to confiscate an April Fool's Day edition of a student newspaper.

By trying to restrict information and ideas, censors undermine one of the primary functions of education: teaching students how to think for themselves. And in denying students exposure to some of the richest works of literature, self-appointed guardians of moral purity are imposing their own narrow views of the world on people at the most impressionable period of their lives. The phenomenon of censorship in the schools means that generations of children may grow up believing that independent thinking is a perilous and even shameful behavior. By discouraging freedom of thought among the young, those who censor are endangering the future of tolerance and free expression in the United States.

Notes

1. Dudley Clendinen, "Fundamentalists Win a Federal Suit Over Schoolbook," *The New York Times*, 25 October 1986.
2. Frances FitzGerald, *America Revised: History Schoolbooks in the Twentieth Century* (Boston: Little, Brown, 1979), p. 10.
3. Dorothy Nelkin, *The Creation Controversy* (New York: Norton, 1982), p.19.
4. Association of American Publishers, American Library Association, and Association for Supervision and Curriculum Development, *Limiting What Students Shall Read* (Washington, DC 1981).
5. Peter Carlson, "Banning Books in the Schools," *The Washington Post Magazine*, 4 January 1987.
6. "Liberty and Learning in the Schools," partial text of speech given by Jean Price, principal of the Church Hill Elementary School in Tennessee and one of the defendants in the *Mozert* case. *Censorship News*, Fall 1987.
7. Lee Burress, *The Battle of the Books: Library Censorship in the Public Schools 1950–1985* (Metuchen, NJ: Scarecrow, 1988).
8. Ronald Glasser, M.D., *365 Days* (New York: George Braziller, 1971).
9. Frances FitzGerald, "A Disagreement in Baileyville," *The New Yorker*, 16 January 1984.
10. Kurt Vonnegut, Jr., "The Idea Killers," *Playboy*, January 1984.
11. Jerry Falwell, *America Can Be Saved*, p.53.
12. Nelkin, p. 63.
13. Mozert et al. v. Hawkins County Public Schools, 647 F.Supp. 1194 E.D. Tenn. (1986); (6th Cir. 1987) review denied 56 U.S.L.W. 3569 (1987).
14. In February 1988 the Supreme Court decided not to hear the evangelical Christians' appeal of the appellate court's ruling, which closed this case but was not expected to end similar challenges to school courses and texts.
15. Smith v. Board of School Commissioners of Mobile County, U.S. Court of Appeals for the Eleventh Circuit (26 August 1987).
16. Edwards v. Aguillard, 55 U.S.L.W. 4860 (19 June 1987).
17. "Return of the Inquisitors," *The Village Voice*, 21 January 1986.

18. "Young America's Foundation Keeps Files on Campus Left," *In These Times*, 23 December 1987.

19. Tinker v. Des Moines School District, 393 U.S. 503 (1969).

20. Bethel School District v. Fraser, 755 F.2d 1356 (9th Cir. 1985), 54 U.S.L.W. 5054 (7 July 1986).

21. Hazelwood School District v. Kuhlmeier, 795 F.2d 1368 (8th Cir. 1986); Supreme Court decision, 13 January 1988.

22. Holmes, Ivan, "Defending Images . . . and the Pursuit of Truth," sidebar accompanying Michael Hoyt, "Look Who's Cracking Down on Press Freedom Now," *Columbia Journalism Review*, March/April 1987.

Selected Readings

American Association of University Professors. *Liberty and Learning in the Nation's Schools. A Report by the Commission on Academic Freedom and Pre-College Education.* Washington, DC: AAUP, 1986.

American Library Association. *Newsletter on Intellectual Freedom* (bimonthly). Chicago: ALA.

Burress, Lee. *The Battle of the Books: Library Censorship in the Public Schools 1950–1985.* Metuchen, NJ: Scarecrow, 1988.

FitzGerald, Frances. *America Revised: History Schoolbooks in the Twentieth Century.* Boston: Little, Brown, 1979.

Jenkinson, Edward. *Censors in the Classroom: The Mind Benders.* Champaign: University of Illinois Press, 1979.

National Coalition Against Censorship. *Books on Trial: A Survey of Recent Cases.* New York: NCAC, 1986.

Nelkin, Dorothy. *The Creation Controversy.* New York: Norton, 1982.

Nelson, Jack. *The Censors and the Schools.* Westport, CT: Greenwood, 1977.

O'Neill, Terry, ed. *Censorship.* St. Paul, MN: Greenhaven, 1985.

PEN American Center. *Right to Read Progress Report* (published periodically). New York: PEN American Center.

People for the American Way. *Attacks on the Freedom to Learn* (annual report on book censorship). Washington, DC: People for the American Way.

Rogers, Donald. *Banned!: Censorship in the Schools.* New York: Messner/Simon and Schuster, 1988.

Student Press Law Center. *Law of the Student Press.* Iowa City: Quill and Scroll, University of Iowa, School of Journalism and Mass Communication, 1986.

Student Press Law Center Report (quarterly). Washington, DC: Student Press Law Center.

3
PRECARIOUS PROSE
The Threat of Libel Suits

In 1980 Richard Hargraves wrote an editorial for the Belleville, Illinois, *News Democrat* criticizing the chairman of the local county board for breaking his campaign promise not to raise taxes. The piece, printed in the paper's "Viewpoint" section, argued that the official "did absolutely nothing to protect your interests" and was "nothing more than another patronage-oriented political hack." The angered official sued for libel; Hargraves and the newspaper were found guilty, and damages of more than $1 million (later reduced to $200,000) were awarded.[1]

This case is one of hundreds brought over the past decade in which journalists, broadcasters, publishers, movie producers, and others have been sued for exercising what they believed was their constitutionally guaranteed right of free expression. No genre of expression has been exempt. Television newscasts, editorials, history books, biographies, and even novels and cartoons have been subjected to libel suits brought by public officials, celebrities, and others who find themselves depicted in ways that displease them. Suits against student publications are also on the rise.[2]

In many instances, enormous sums are at stake. Since 1980 juries have awarded libel plaintiffs damages of $1 million or more in at least thirty cases. A 1984 study by the Libel Defense Resource Center found that the average jury award for libel damages was triple that allowed in product liability and medical malpractice cases.

Libel is defined as communication—words or pictures—that tends to expose someone to public ridicule, shame, or contempt, or otherwise damages a person's reputation. Traditionally, severe penalties have been imposed for libel, in recognition of the embarrassment and possible loss of income associated with defamatory statements.

Some libel cases have a degree of legitimacy, such as the suit of actress Carol Burnett against the *National Enquirer* for a story falsely reporting that she had been drunk and disorderly in public. However, libel suits are frequently brought for reasons that are, at best, tangential to the protection of someone's reputation. Some plaintiffs have political aims or are interested in discouraging or punishing unfavorable coverage; others may simply be fishing for damage awards.

Even in those cases in which the allegations of libel are found to be without merit, libel suits are costly to defend. In this climate it is not surprising that many publishers and broadcasters have become particularly cautious about the content of what they produce. Libel lawyers are consulted more frequently, and media executives are demonstrating a tendency to avoid potential problems by toning down controversial material—especially investigative reporting—or "spiking" it altogether.[3]

While this trend toward self-censorship is difficult to measure, there is no doubt that it has deprived the public of valuable news and information. Simply the threat of a libel suit has intimidated many members of the Fourth Estate and the resulting atmosphere has shifted discussion of controversial issues from public forums to the courts. This "chilly" climate in effect creates a type of immunity for powerful public figures.[4] The overall result is a crippling of free and open discourse.

From Sedition to Sullivan

We'd better tone this down or George III will sue us for libel.
—Caption of cartoon by Auth of the *Philadelphia Inquirer*, April 20, 1985, showing Revolutionary War leaders looking at the Declaration of Independence

Although libel is regarded today as an issue that involves celebrities and individual public figures, the origins of the concept are bound up with the right to criticize the government. In pre-Revolutionary America, colonial authorities frequently used laws prohibiting "seditious libel" to squelch dissent.

These statutes, based on British jurisprudence, mandated harsh penalties for any statement that was deemed to be defamatory, even if it was true. The rule went unchallenged until 1735, when the lawyer defending printer John Peter Zenger, who had published a statement criticizing the unpopular governor of New York, successfully persuaded a jury that Zenger should not be convicted if the published statement was found to be accurate. In acquitting Zenger—and rejecting the existing law—the jury helped establish the principle of a free press in America.

While the Zenger verdict bolstered the country's spirit of independence, it did not rapidly transform the law of libel. In fact, even well into the twentieth century libel remained an offense of "strict liability" in most states, meaning that the truth defense had to overcome a heavy presumption of injury.

The doctrine of seditious libel resurfaced in the new nation with the Sedition Act of 1798. A deliberate attempt by the Federalist Party to suppress opposition to its programs, the act made it a crime to publish "false, scandalous, and malicious writing or writings against the United States, or either house of the Congress . . . or the President."

Once the law was passed, leaders of the Adams administration moved to enforce it against written and oral statements of the Republicans. Threats were issued, and editors were jailed.

The Sedition Act expired after two years, but opposition to government policies remained punishable under a succession of congressional statutes, presidential orders, and court decisions.

The U.S. system remained ambiguous about the extent to which it was permissible for citizens to criticize the government. James Madison advocated uninhibited public debate, regarding it as the best means of arriving at an accurate assessment of the state of the nation. Thomas Jefferson, who spoke against the crime of seditious libel when he was out of office, voiced no objection when it was used against those who criticized him during his presidency. Justice Oliver Wendell Holmes, who wrote stirring and profound opinions on First Amendment freedoms, rationalized the use of the Sedition Act of 1918 to imprison the socialist Eugene Debs for his speeches advocating resistance to military conscription for World War I.

Thus, for nearly two centuries after the founding of the country, state and federal libel laws remained in place to discourage blunt criticism of elected officials. The Supreme Court sanctioned them, ruling as late as 1942 that libelous statements, along with obscenity and "fighting words," fell outside the protection of the First Amendment.[5]

All this changed in 1964, when the Court ruled on a libel complaint brought against *The New York Times* by a police commissioner in Montgomery, Alabama. L. B. Sullivan had sought $500,000 in damages in connection with an advertisement published in the *Times* on March 29, 1960, by civil rights leaders and activists who were seeking to draw attention to the desegregation battles then raging in the South. The ad noted that student leaders had been expelled from schools and "loads of police armed with shotguns and tear gas ringed the Alabama state college campus."

Though Sullivan was not mentioned by name, he claimed to be identifiable, and thus defamed, in his role as Montgomery police commissioner. But Sullivan's chief complaint was broader than anything that could be called libel. As an ardent segregationist, he was hostile to the media, which were helping to make the civil rights movement a burning national issue. His lawsuit against the *Times*, which won success under the laws of Alabama, was intended to discourage press coverage of the struggle for desegregation.

In a landmark decision, the Supreme Court overturned the *Times*'s conviction in the lower courts and rejected the Alabama libel law. The Court ruled that Sullivan could not prevail against the newspaper even if the ad contained inaccuracies (which it did), unless the newspaper itself was shown to have had reckless disregard for the accuracy of the statements it published. A free and robust press, the Court said, needed to operate without fear of being prosecuted and incurring heavy legal fees each time an error was made.[6]

The Sullivan case was clearly of extraordinary importance to the civil rights movement, and it continues to be of unparalleled significance for the free press.[7] Yet the decision failed to answer a diverse array of relevant questions. How, for example, could it be proven that a publication acted in "reckless disregard" of the truth? Did this standard apply to all libel plaintiffs, or only to public officials? What difference would it make if the alleged defamation was contained in a news article, a cartoon, or a novel?

In subsequent years, the Court at first seemed to raise the level of protection for media libel defendants. The "reckless disregard" standard established for Sullivan, a public official, was ruled to apply also to public figures. Then it was established that private citizens who alleged libel carried a lesser burden, and needed only to show that the journalist (or writer, filmmaker, etc.) had been negligent. But how could it be determined whether one was a public or a private figure? The major difference, the Court said, depended on the extent to which the disputed media coverage was voluntary or involuntary, and on the allegedly defamed person's ability to respond through the media, short of going to court.

Other Supreme Court decisions have made the press more vulnerable to libel actions. Especially disheartening was a 1979 ruling that gave libel plaintiffs access to editorial notes, records of reporters' conversations, and other material that might be relevant to a finding of reckless disregard. This single decision made libel suits far more expensive and time-consuming to defend. Many weeks are now necessary before trial in order to review the material furnished by both sides. In this process the meticulous journalist who has kept extensive notes may encounter particular difficulty because he or she must supply such documents to the other side during pretrial discovery proceedings. At the same time, pressure is exerted on the reporter to reveal the identities of confidential sources. The dynamics of the process have made libel suits attractive to those plaintiffs who seek to attack the credibility of particular publications or journalists.

Where Libel Litigation Is Alive and Well

Despite the Sullivan ruling, the use of libel laws by public officials to challenge the media has flourished at the state and local levels. One hot spot has been Philadelphia, where as many as fifteen libel suits at a time have been brought by former mayors, judges, prosecutors, and even a member of Congress. The *Philadelphia Inquirer* is perhaps the most besieged paper in the country. During the 1980s, its reporters and editors have spent innumerable and costly hours on libel litigation and suffered jury awards as high as $4 million.

In 1987 a television station in Mobile, Alabama, was sued for $5 million by the president of the county commission. At issue was a newscast in which the station had presented footage of a public hearing. One of the participants in the hearing had made false assertions, which the station recognized and took care to rebut in follow-up statements. Nonetheless, a state court ruled the broadcast libelous.

National figures sometimes try to use state libel laws to their advantage. In 1984 then Senator Paul Laxalt of Nevada filed a $250 million suit against McClatchy Newspapers for an article reporting that profits had been skimmed from a casino at a time when Laxalt was its principal owner. McClatchy viewed the action as an attempt to deter the rest of the media from pursuing the story and filed a countersuit. Soon after a federal judge ruled in April 1987 that the writer of the story did not have to reveal his sources, the two parties settled the suit; Laxalt received no damages.

Even when libel complaints are settled out of court or are decided in favor of the defendants, the sheer time and expense required to prepare a defense often has a chilling effect on future coverage.[8] In addition to the phenomenon of self-censorship, a publication that has been sued for libel may also find it more difficult to gain access to newsmakers and sources. A newspaper or other media outlet that has been sued for libel may find that regardless of the outcome it has been made into a pariah.

Even at the federal level, the Sullivan decision has not completely protected the media from attack. Under the rubric of national security the government has frequently attempted to punish the press for reporting embarrassing or sensitive information (see chapter 9).

The direct use of libel laws also has been employed by former government officials. For instance, David Atlee Phillips, a former CIA official, sued Donald Freed and Fred Landis, authors of *A Death in Washington*, and their publisher, Lawrence Hill & Company, for $210 million for linking him to the Washington murder of former Chilean ambassador Orlando Letelier.[9] Phillips also used the popular "national security" argument in refusing to answer questions from defense attorneys during the pretrial discovery process.[10] The case was settled out of court after the authors agreed to retract the allegations against Phillips publicly.

The ability of the government and former officials to hide behind rationales like "national security" puts into question the entire legitimacy of libel laws with respect to public figures. In fact, some critics have called for what amounts to a deregulation of political speech through the abolition of the right of public officials to bring libel suits.[11]

Lancing the Press

The attempt by journalists to defend themselves against the growing wave of libel actions has been inhibited by a strong public displeasure with various media practices. Libel plaintiffs often win popular support because they reinforce the notion that the press is an arrogant, monolithic institution guilty of sensationalism for the sake of profit, the glorification of gossip, and the invasion of individual privacy. The status and glamour that the press, particularly investigative reporters, enjoyed in the wake of the Watergate affair have receded greatly during the conservative national political atmosphere of the 1980s.

The extent to which investigative journalism is under siege was demonstrated in a suit against the Alton, Illinois, *Telegraph*, after two of its reporters sent a confidential memo to federal law enforcement officials; the memo contained information about a local builder who was suspected of having links to organized crime. Although this information was never published, the memo made its way to the Federal Home Loan Bank, and as a result the builder's line of credit was cut off. Apprised of the memo, he sued for libel and was initially awarded $9.2 million in damages. The *Telegraph* subsequently went into Chapter 11 bankruptcy as a result of the high legal fees and is now under new management. Both of the reporters involved in the case have left the newspaper, which is now less inclined to do investigative reporting.[12]

As the Illinois Hargraves case indicated, newspapers have been prosecuted for editorial opinion as well as for statements of fact, and this offers perhaps the clearest indication of how libel suits strike at the heart of a free press. The danger was anticipated by James Madison in an attack on the Sedition Act:

> It must be obvious to the plainest minds, that opinions and inferences, and conjectural observations, are not only in many cases inseparable from the facts, but may often be more the objects of prosecution than the facts themselves.[13]

News stories and editorials are not the only categories of journalism to be hit with the libel weapon. The *Chicago Tribune* and its architecture writer were sued by real estate developer Donald Trump for poking fun at his ambition to build the world's tallest building. Cartoonist Paul Szep of *The Boston Globe* has been sued for libel some half-dozen times in his career; a $3.6 million suit against him was filed by former Massachusetts governor Edward King. In a case that went all the way to the Supreme Court, fundamentalist preacher Jerry Falwell sued *Hustler* magazine for a satirical feature. The issue at stake was whether Falwell could claim damages for "emotional distress" even though the jury had found that the satire—a tasteless parody of a liquor ad that depicted Falwell as a drunkard having sex with his mother in an outhouse—was not libelous because it was in no way believable. The high court was not sufficiently swayed by Falwell's embarrassment. In February 1988 the justices voted 8 to 0 in favor of *Hustler* and gave a ringing endorsement of the right to criticize public figures, even if it involves statements that are "outrageous" or offensive.

Rewriting History in the Courts

It was in 1984 that two of the most momentous libel trials of the age got under way, both in New York City. The first case was brought by retired General William Westmoreland against CBS in response to a television documentary that charged that Westmoreland, during his tenure as commander of U.S. troops in Vietnam, allowed falsified intelligence data on the war to be sent to his superiors at the Pentagon. Although evidence indicated that the journalistic standards of the CBS documentary were sometimes questionable, Westmoreland dropped the suit before a verdict was reached.

The other case was a $50 million suit brought by Israeli general Ariel Sharon against *Time* magazine for the way it had depicted his connection to the massacre by Lebanese Phalangist soldiers of hundreds of Palestinian civilians.

In this case, too, there were revelations of sloppy journalistic practices. But both Westmoreland and Sharon had a larger purpose than protecting their reputations and correcting factual errors. Civil libertarians agreed that both cases were deliberately designed to attract major media coverage with the aim of trying to remold public opinion regarding two highly disputed subjects: U.S. involvement in Vietnam and the Israeli invasion of Lebanon. Westmoreland and his financial backers, including several New Right organizations, clearly hoped to revise the public record on the failure of the military to assess the deterioration of its position in Vietnam adequately. Sharon hoped to obscure the fact that an Israeli commission had found him "indirectly responsible" for the massacres at Sabra and El Shatila. In both cases the plaintiffs were seeking to use the libel laws to rewrite history.

Some plaintiffs seek to draw attention away from critical accounts of their actions by bringing libel charges based on an incidental personal issue. Perhaps the most celebrated instance of this sort was the case brought against Peter Matthiessen for his book *In the Spirit of Crazy Horse,* which deals with the confrontation that took place between government officials and Native American activists in South Dakota in the 1970s. Angered at statements about him in the book, South Dakota governor William Janklow sued the author and his publisher, Viking, for libel, asking for $25 million in damages. The complaint focused on Matthiessen's references to old allegations that Janklow had raped a young Indian girl during his time as a legal services attorney on the Rosebud Indian Reservation. The rumors had been in circulation since 1967 and had been considered and dismissed by the FBI, which Matthiessen also noted.

Janklow sued not only Matthiessen and Viking but also *Newsweek* for mentioning the charges in an article it had carried about *In the Spirit of Crazy Horse.* In addition, Janklow personally telephoned booksellers in several states, threatening to sue them as well unless they stopped selling the book; he actually did bring suit against several bookstores in South Dakota. The inclusion of the booksellers greatly expanded the potential impact of this case; no court, however, has been willing to accept the argument that booksellers have a responsibility to vouch for the accuracy of their inventory.

Matthiessen and Viking were also hit with a $25 million libel suit brought by David Price, an FBI agent who claimed that *In the Spirit of Crazy Horse* defamed him. In January 1988 a federal district court dismissed that suit, ruling that authors have a right to publish "an entirely one-sided view of people and events." Judge Diana E. Murphy gave judicial endorsement to writing on controversial subjects by holding that "speech about government and its officers, about how well or badly they carry out their duties, lies at the very heart of the First Amendment." In 1989 Janklow's suit was also dismissed by a judge who found that Matthiessen had not shown reckless disregard of the truth.

Libel as Intimidation

During the last ten years, for every relatively legitimate libel suit, dozens have been intended purely to intimidate. Cult organizations are especially fond of this tactic. Lyndon La-Rouche, Synanon, and the Church of Scientology all have brought aggressive libel suits clearly aimed at discouraging press coverage of their activities.

LaRouche, a onetime leftist who veered to the extreme right, brought a $20 million suit against the publisher of a small New York City weekly called *Our Town* and its reporter Dennis King, who had written a series of investigative articles about LaRouche entitled "Nazis on the Rise." Though the case was dismissed, King says that the very fact that it was brought, along with numerous other libel suits by LaRouche, have made it difficult to find publishers who will buy articles about him and his organization.

In 1984, as NBC was about to air a program about LaRouche, he attempted to suppress it by filing a $100 million libel suit in federal court against the network, several staffers, Dennis King, the Anti-Defamation League of B'nai B'rith, and others who had helped in preparing the piece. During months of trial preparation, LaRouche's people engaged in various forms of harassment, including picketing against an NBC reporter and claiming she was a prostitute, and distributing a bogus newspaper to King's neighbors—with his photo on the front page—that maligned his sexual practices. The court found the suit to be an entirely frivolous attempt to intimidate reporters and, after a countersuit filed by NBC, ordered LaRouche to pay several million dollars in damages.

In another incident, Synanon sent some 1,000 letters to wire services, publishers, and broadcasters, threatening to take legal action if corrections were not made regarding virtually every story printed about the organization in 1978 and 1979. During this period, Synanon members were being tried for attempted murder after a rattlesnake had been placed in the mailbox of an attorney involved in a suit against Synanon.

Small and alternative publishers are especially vulnerable to this sort of threat. The Jackson, Mississippi, *Advocate* was hit with a libel suit by the National Alliance Party, an action the paper believes was a deliberate attempt to put it out of business.

Libel actions meant to intimidate also have been brought by people and organizations who are considered quite reputable. Landlords have sued tenants for statements made about them, and employers have sued their employees. In a case that reached the Supreme Court, the owner of Bill Johnson's Restaurants in Phoenix filed a libel charge in relation to leaflets that had been distributed on a picket line organized by waitresses who were calling attention to what they said were management's mistreatment of employees and "unwarranted sexual advances." The case was dismissed in the lower courts as a thinly veiled effort to prevent workers from engaging in legitimate collective activity, but when it reached the Supreme Court it was reinstated on the grounds that employers were entitled to their day in court.[14]

The Court's decision in this case has given a green light to employers who seek to suppress the free speech of labor. In one instance libel charges were brought against a group of workers at the American Motors Corporation plant in Kenosha, Wisconsin, who were issuing a newsletter called *Fighting Times*. The $4.2 million suit was brought by company foremen who were criticized in the publication, but it was later revealed to have been paid for by American Motors.

Celebrity Suits and Libelous Fiction

An inevitable result of the boom in reporting and book publishing about celebrities has been an expansion in the number of libel suits. Cases brought by subjects of "juicy" articles, books, and broadcasts who did not like the way they were portrayed have become a staple of entertainment news. It is tempting to believe that many of these suits are brought solely to elicit even more publicity for the subject, but they can set dangerous legal precedents. Perhaps most disturbing was the threat by Frank Sinatra to sue author Kitty Kelley *before* she began writing a biography of him.

Legal conflicts can arise even when the subject is collaborating with the author. A striking example involves a $15 million action brought by Jeffrey Macdonald, who was convicted in the late 1970s of the murder of his wife and two children. While he was appealing the conviction, Macdonald looked for someone to write his story and signed a contract with the writer Joe McGinniss. Although it was not stated in the contract, Macdonald assumed that McGinniss would support his claim of innocence in the murders.

McGinniss, however, reached a different conclusion in the book *Fatal Vision*, which became a bestseller and the basis for a television miniseries. Macdonald sued McGinniss, alleging fraud, emotional distress, and other injuries. In August 1987 the suit ended in a mistrial when jurors failed, after twenty hours of deliberation, to agree on a verdict. Later that year the case was settled for $325,000. Macdonald told reporters that he felt vindicated, while the lawyer for McGinniss insisted that his client's book stood "untarnished."

People also have brought suits charging that they were libeled by works of fiction. For example, a California psychologist who conducted nude encounter sessions was awarded $75,000 in damages from a novelist who had participated in one of these sessions and later wrote a fictionalized account of it. Courts in different states, however, have differed as to the merit of such actions. A New York court, considering the complaint of a writer's former girlfriend, found no basis for her claim that she had been libeled in his novel.

The problem with such suits is that they pose a great threat to the creative process. Most works of fiction bear at least some resemblance to the writer's personal experiences, which, after all, is the raw material of literature. How, then, can the appropriate degree of attention be paid to individual reputation without stifling creativity? As Judge Irving Kaufman has written:

> Simply according artistic works the same protection as nonartistic works may not be sufficient to protect creativity. After all, the very essence of artistic expression is invention and artists necessarily draw on their own experience. But if the rules of liability are unclear, artists will not be able to know how much disguise is sufficient to protect their claims from the claims of those who may see themselves in the portrayals.[15]

It's sometimes difficult to understand why plaintiffs go to the trouble of bringing libel suits. The initial indignation at reading what is considered a scurrilous article or book or broadcast is understandable. But given the mixed record of libel litigation, potential plaintiffs have little reason to believe they will be totally vindicated. In the quest for what is likely to be at best a partial court victory, plaintiffs spend huge amounts of time and money, which, in light of the fact that most large jury awards are later reduced on appeal by more than seventy-five percent, are unlikely to be recovered even if a plaintiff wins.

Whether or not libel litigation provides satisfaction to plaintiffs, the fact that the phenomenon is so widespread has created a troubling challenge to free speech. The Supreme Court ruling in the Falwell case was encouraging. Cartoonist Garry Trudeau was so pleased that he drew in a Supreme Court seal of approval on a Doonesbury strip that ridiculed the recently disclosed sexual indiscretions of Jimmy Swaggart.

Yet the ruling does not remove the threat posed by the use of libel suits to intimidate. As long as we have libel laws that allow public figures to drag their critics into court, free speech will remain inhibited. As Martin Garbus, Floyd Abrams, and other legal experts in the field have argued, significant changes in libel litigation procedures are needed to remove the curbs on public discourse imposed by rampant libel suits.

Notes

1. Hargraves served several days in jail for his refusal to disclose the names of confidential sources.

2. See "Liability and the Student Press," *Student Press Law Center Report*, Fall 1985, p. 29.

3. Robert Picard, "Self-Censorship Threatens U.S. Press Freedom," *Index on Censorship*, March 1982.

4. See Michael Massing's analysis of libel trends in "The Libel Chill: How Cold Is It Out There?" *Columbia Journalism Review*, May/June 1985.

5. Chaplinsky v. New Hampshire, 315 U.S. 568 (1942).

6. The New York Times v. Sullivan, 376 U.S. 254 (1964).

7. A fuller treatment of the Sullivan case and its importance can be found in Anthony Lewis, "Annals of Law: The Sullivan Case," *The New Yorker*, 5 November 1984.

8. Floyd Abrams, "Why We Should Change Libel Law," *The New York Times Magazine*, 29 September 1985, p. 34.

9. This action was paid for by an organization formed in 1981 to finance suits by former intelligence agents. See Eve Pell, "Taking C.I.A. Critics to Court," *The Nation*, 17 October 1981.

10. Jack Anderson, "When Spies Go to Court," *The Washington Post*, 12 June 1983.

11. Gilbert Cranberg, "Burying the Libel Hatchet," *Washington Journalism Review*, January/February 1988; Martin Garbus, "Abolish Libel—The Only Answer," *The Nation*, 8 October 1983.

12. Cindy Skaugen, "A Profitable, yet Cautious *Telegraph*," *The State Journal-Register* (Springfield, IL), 12 May 1985.

13. *Elliot's Debates on the Federal Constitution*, vol. 4, p. 575.

14. Nat Hentoff, "Libel and Labor, Bill Johnson's Restaurant Serves Up a Chill," *The Progressive*, November 1983.

15. Irving R. Kaufman, "The Creative Process and Libel," *The New York Times Magazine*, 5 April 1987.

Selected Readings

Bezanson, Randall, Gilbert Cranberg, and John Soloski. *Libel Law and the Press: Myth and Reality.* New York: The Free Press/ Macmillan, 1987.

Garbus, Martin. *Traitors and Heroes.* New York: Atheneum, 1987.

Littlewood, Thomas B., *Coals of Fire: The Alton Telegraph Libel Case.* Carbondale: Southern Illinois University Press, 1988.

Smith, Jeffrey. *The Printers and Press Freedom.* New York: Oxford University Press, 1988.

Smolla, Rodney A. *Suing The Press: Libel, The Media and Power.* New York: Oxford University Press, 1986.

Student Press Law Center, *Law of the Student Press.* Iowa City: Quill and Scroll, University of Iowa, School of Journalism and Mass Communication, 1986. Chapter on libel, pp. 31–38.

Student Press Law Center. Student Press Law Center Report, vol. 4, no. 3, "Malice." Iowa City: Quill and Scroll, University of Iowa, School of Journalism and Mass Communication, 1985.

4

THE GUARDIANS OF DECENCY

The Pornography Debate in the Print, Broadcast, and Music Industries

My concept? You can't do anything *with anybody's body to make it dirty to me. Six people, eight people, one person— you can do only one thing to make it dirty: kill it.*
— Lenny Bruce[1]

In 1986 North Carolina enacted a law that makes it a felony for adults to view erotic material—even in their own homes. At about the same time, it was reported that the mayor of Scottsdale, Arizona, had urged local residents to supply police with the license-plate numbers of people seen entering movie theaters showing X-rated films. At the federal level, the FBI, the Postal Service, and the Justice Department have all launched "antiporn" campaigns involving prosecutions, steep fines, and the confiscation of property.

The bluenoses are back, and they are stronger than ever. During the 1980s a great many groups have launched an ambitious assault on what they consider obscenity in books, magazines, films, records, videos, and virtually any other medium found to offend their various standards of decency. From the National Federation for Decency to the Moral Majority, such self-appointed crusaders for propriety found sympathetic ears in local governments as well as in the Reagan administration. Such groups, which regard organized opposition against obscenity as a component of their conservative social agenda, have also forged an unlikely alliance with some feminists who support the suppression of pornography as a step toward ending the degradation of women.

Smut-busting is not peculiar to our time. For more than a century there have been efforts to rid the nation of sexually explicit images. The difference today is that "antiporn" forces no longer limit their battle to small-time purveyors of dirty pictures plying their trade in back alleys. In an era when erotic products and images are all around us and sex is used to sell everything from motor oil to mouthwash, the crusaders are a growing influence throughout society. They are particularly concerned, of course, with explicit sexual messages, and indeed there are plenty of those; "Dial-A-Porn" telephone services alone account for a billion-dollar trade, and even greater profits are derived from "adult" printed matter, films, and videos that are readily available in most parts of the country.

For some the rise in the volume and relative openness of the sex business is a healthy sign of a breakdown in social taboos, an offshoot of the so-called sexual revolution. Others regard it as an indication that growing numbers of people—daunted by confusing sexual mores and the risk of fatal disease—are opting for fantasy rather than the real thing. Still others see it as part of a general decay of moral standards.

Whatever the reason, there is no question that what amounts to a powerful pornography-bashing backlash raises serious threats to individual liberties. Surely some materials might elicit abhorrence from almost everyone—those involving graphic depictions of violence, for example—yet there is no practical way of drawing the line.

What is more troubling is that many of the moral crusaders do not stop at the most offensive cases. Their range of targets is much wider, and their efforts amount to a frightening assault on freedom of expression and individual privacy. The fight against pornography inevitably turns into a campaign for another form of censorship.

From Homer to Comstock

[Aphrodite] spoke and loosened from her bosom the embroidered girdle of many colors into which all her allurements were fashioned. In it was love and in it desire and in it blandishing persuasion which steals the mind even of the wise.
—Homer, *The Iliad*, Book XIV, translated by Richard Lattimore

For centuries, sexuality and nudity were conventional ingredients of great works of art and popular entertainment. The writings of Aristophanes, Boccaccio, Chaucer, and Rabelais, to name a few, contained healthy doses of bawdiness. The paintings of Raphael, Titian, Rubens, and many other artists openly depicted the undraped human form.

The urge to censor such works emerged in the seventeenth century. In Puritan England, bodily pleasure was branded sinful and immoral. Even then, laws against obscenity evolved slowly in the Anglo-Saxon world. It was only with the spread of printed matter that the guardians of morality became worried about what would happen if material they considered objectionable fell into the hands of the masses. The first anti-obscenity legislation enacted in England was adopted in 1824; it prohibited exposing an obscene book or print in public places. By 1857, in what became known as the Campbell Act, English law prohibited the dissemination of all obscene materials.

In the New World, all thirteen colonies made blasphemy or profanity a criminal offense, yet only Massachusetts had a law, passed in 1712, prohibiting the circulation of sexually explicit material. Linking profane speech to religious heresy, it outlawed the "composing, writing, printing, or publishing of any filthy, obscene, or profane song, pamphlet, libel, or mock sermon in imitation or mimicking of religious services."[2]

During the first half of the nineteenth century, many states adopted laws to deal with obscene works. The first federal anti-obscenity statute, aimed at halting the importation of lurid postcards, was adopted in 1842. In 1865, in response to concerns that soldiers had been corrupted by "dirty" literature during the Civil War, Congress passed the first law prohibiting the sending of obscene materials through the mails.

At about this time, Anthony Comstock,[3] a former grocery clerk, embarked on what would be a forty-year career as the nation's leading crusader against vice. Assisted by the YMCA, he formed the Society for the Suppression of Vice to lobby for stringent state and national anti-obscenity legislation, a campaign that led Congress to pass an omnibus anti-obscenity bill in 1873: the Comstock Law. Comstock himself was made a special agent of the Post Office in charge of enforcing the statute. His less than savory tactics included the use of informers and decoys and the harassment of birth-control reformers.[4]

By 1900 some thirty states had adopted companion anti-obscenity legislation. It is interesting to note that the laissez-faire notions of the age did not extend to this area. Comstock's vice squads, crusading under the banner of "Morals, Not Art or Literature," were supported by wealthy individuals—including financier J. P. Morgan—many of whom had their own private collections of erotica.

Aside from their concern for morality, the crusaders for decency of that era (like those today) expressed concern about those they considered to be harmed by the disputed material. Until the 1950s many books, plays, films, and other works of art were suppressed under the Hicklin doctrine, derived from a nineteenth-century British case that judged obscenity by the "effect of isolated passages upon the most susceptible persons."[5]

By the 1920s the mood of social progress in the country made the actions of antivice groups less popular. On one particular front, the American literary community became impatient at the policy of the U.S. Customs Bureau that barred from United States shores the works of such classic authors as Balzac, Voltaire, and Rousseau and newer writers like D. H. Lawrence and James Joyce.

In 1933, Bennett Cerf of Random House tested an eleven-year ban on Joyce's *Ulysses* by arranging to have a copy sent to him from abroad. The ensuing trial resulted in a landmark decision by Federal Judge John Woolsey that overturned the ban. While he noted that *Ulysses* was a difficult work that might not appeal to all tastes, Woolsey stated, "I have not found anything that I consider to be dirt for dirt's sake."

Shortly after this, the Catholic Church established the National Office for Decent Literature, which circulated monthly lists of books it considered indecent. The authors whom subscribers were warned to avoid included celebrated writers like John Dos Passos and William Faulkner. During the same period the film industry set up the Hays Office to enforce stricter moral standards in movies. Nevertheless, the government generally reduced its activities as the ultimate guardian of decency.[6]

Sexual Explicitness Expands

This is not to say that the obscenity issue was dead. In *Roth v. U.S.* in 1957 the Supreme Court set regulation in this area on a new course with a decision restating the application of the First

Amendment to sexually explicit material. Since nudity and other titillating images did not necessarily create a "clear and present danger"—the only exception under which otherwise constitutionally protected expression could be enjoined—the Court needed some other basis, which it found by declaring obscenity totally outside the range of speech encompassed by the First Amendment.

Obscene expression, the Court ruled, was material that had no redeeming social value. However, the Court made it clear that this was to be a very limited category, much narrower than the "weakest person" Hicklin standard. The portrayal of sex and obscenity were not to be considered synonymous; indeed, the Court said, "sex, a great and mysterious motive force in human life, has indisputably been a subject of absorbing interest." Only what it defined as true obscenity—speech that was considered totally worthless—could be suppressed.

After this ruling, judicial tolerance for the censorship of erotic material declined greatly. In 1959, a court lifted the thirty-year ban on D. H. Lawrence's *Lady Chatterley's Lover*. By 1966, when a Massachusetts ban on the erotic novel *Fanny Hill* was reversed, many observers concluded that the 1957 Supreme Court ruling made it all but impossible to prosecute for obscenity, except when material was sold to minors.[7] Nonetheless, some controversial figures suffered harassment. In the early 1960s comedian Lenny Bruce was repeatedly arrested and charged with obscenity by local authorities because of his ribald night-club acts.

That decade as a whole produced a growing degree of tolerance for—not to mention demand for—greater openness in artistic and personal expression. Freedom from sexual inhibitions was a major theme of the day, one that became inseparable from the alternative political initiatives that were also burgeoning.

Sex and politics were joined in the underground press. Many publications that started out focusing on politics soon found that perhaps the only way to survive was to include sexual content in their editorial material, as well as candid personal ads. Sometimes the sex overwhelmed the politics, as when Jim Buckley, the leftist editor of the *New York Free Press*, joined publisher Al Goldstein to start *Screw* magazine, which he called "the Consumer's Report of Sex."[8] It boosted its circulation to 100,000 by publishing graphic articles about masturbation and homosexuality, interviews with prostitutes, and unrestrained displays of human anatomy. Its taste was often questionable, and *Screw* helped set a new standard of immodesty among openly sold publications.

Backlash and the 1967 Pornography Commission

Not everyone welcomed the unhibited new atmosphere. Pro-decency forces around the country regrouped and exerted pressure on the federal government to limit what they regarded as a flood of smut circulating in schools, stores, homes, and in the mails. In 1967 Congress responded with legislation that established a National Commission on Pornography.

The Commission was given two principal tasks: to research the causal relationship between sexually explicit materials and antisocial behavior, and to recommend effective and constitutional ways of addressing any negative consequences of this material.[9] From the outset, research was given priority. Despite widespread public debate about the "porn problem," little formal attempt had been made to discover what Americans actually thought about this issue.

The methods employed by the Commission included gathering statistical information on the circulation of erotic literature; undertaking surveys of attitudes and experiences related to consumption; and conducting controlled psychological experiments to study community norms.

After two years of research, the Commission arrived at conclusions that came as a major disappointment to the anti-pornography crusaders. First, it found that much of the problem regarding sexual images was not based in the material but rather stemmed "from the inability or reluctance of people in our society to be open and direct in dealing with sexual matters." Moreover, one of the Commission's major public opinion surveys indicated that only two percent of Americans viewed sexually explicit material as a significant social problem. Because of its broadly worded questions, the survey drew considerable criticism.

The Commission found other signs that most Americans were not offended by sexually explicit material, though the results showed that many were concerned about its effects on others. Most of those surveyed saw little need for additional obscenity laws, and those who thought otherwise expressed the view that such laws could not be enforced. And many said they had found in erotic material a valuable source of information about sex.

The Commission also analyzed public responses to questions about the impact of erotic material. In many instances the fears that had been expressed by the antipornography groups were not sustained by the experiences of those interviewed. For example, while more than fifty percent of people said they believed that sexual material could lead someone to commit rape or other antisocial acts, when asked about themselves and people they knew, most people could cite no specific incidents to justify their beliefs.

From answers such as these the Commission arrived at the conclusion that there was no consensus about the effects of erotic materials. As if challenging antipornography advocates to produce hard data, it noted:

> Interestingly, persons who envision undesirable effects rarely or never report having personally experienced them, are more likely to say they occurred to someone else, and are most likely to simply believe in the effect occurring without reference either to themselves or to anyone they personally know.[10]

The Commission's recommended solutions to the controversy focused on the need for better sex education, better communication about sexual matters, and additional research. More anti-obscenity laws were not the answer, it stated. Indeed, the Commission called for the repeal of existing statutes, except for those concerning children.

Most government officials were not pleased with these conclusions. Many members of Congress, along with President Nixon and other conservatives, loudly rejected the Commission's report. As a result, no obscenity statutes were repealed; on the contrary, not long after the report was issued, Congress approved an amendment to the Postal Reorganization Act that prohibited the mailing of sexually oriented commercial advertising to persons who indicated they did not want it.

The next important development in the field occurred in 1973, when the Supreme Court made yet another attempt to define obscenity as a form of speech that fell outside the province of constitutional protection. In a case that remains the standard, Marvin Miller, a major publisher of pornography, was convicted of violating California law by distributing unsolicited obscene materials through the mail. He appealed to the Supreme Court, arguing that the law was unconstitutional.

In a 5 to 4 decision, the Court refused to hold that all state obscenity laws violated the First Amendment. Instead, it established a new three-part test based on community standards for states and localities to use in determining whether material is obscene.[11]

Since 1973, innumerable attempts have been made by local authorities to exercise the new authority granted under the *Miller* standard. But many of them came up against a 1974 Supreme Court ruling in a case that involved an attempt to suppress the film *Carnal Knowledge:* Local juries did not have "unbridled discretion" in deciding what was obscene and such a determination could be applied only to material depicting "patently offensive hard-core sexual conduct."

Obviously, the standards remained somewhat unclear, and so the battles continued to rage. They also spread to different arenas as erotic material found its way into new communications media. With satellite-transmitted television, sex flies through space; with Dial-A-Porn services it comes through the phone lines; and with erotic computer games like Leather Goddesses of Phobos it pops up in the home PC.

Tipper Gore Versus Jello Biafra

The self-appointed forces of decency also have to contend with the fact that sexual content is on the rise even in mainstream channels of communication like network television. Prime-time programs such as *Dallas, Dynasty,* and *Miami Vice,* as well as daytime soap operas, are filled with verbal and visual sexual innuendos. In other programs, such as *Cagney and Lacey,* the plots are deliberately constructed to raise such social issues as infidelity and contraception; this approach has gained credibility and popularity as a result of public concern about AIDS and teenage pregnancy.[12] In an effort to educate viewers, public service ads have sometimes been even more sexually explicit. The trend toward "permissiveness" has also been seen in rock music, films, and most other dimensions of cultural life.

Once again the slide toward openness has been accompanied by a resurgence of antipornography activism. One of the most successful crusaders of recent vintage is Tipper Gore, the founder of the Parents Music Resource Center. Gore has effectively used her position as the wife of a U.S. senator in her campaign against what she regards as socially harmful lyrics in rock music. Acting on her homespun analysis, she is seeking to shield children from what she and her supporters believe is a major cause of teenage suicide, the breakup of families, and a litany of other social problems.[13]

Largely because Gore solicited the participation of fifteen other congressional spouses, she was able to arrange a special congressional hearing on rock lyrics and to pressure the music industry into agreeing to place warning labels on records with explicit sexual lyrics. After this success Gore expanded the scope of her campaign to include music videos, television programs, and videocassettes.

Gore argues that her efforts do not amount to censorship, that her aim is simply a rating system like the one that is in effect in the motion picture industry. (That system has not been flawless: Numerous filmmakers have been forced to tone down or delete footage in order to avoid X or R ratings, since theater owners in some parts of the country refuse to display movies with those designations.)

The introduction of warning labels for music already has had repercussions for performers, some of whom have been forced to modify lyrics and album art.[14] Gore has also helped create a climate in which musicians can be prosecuted. In 1986 Jello Biafra, lead singer of the Dead Kennedys, a politically oriented punk band, was charged with violating a California law prohibiting the distribution of materials harmful to minors. The alleged offense was the enclosure, in the album *Frankenchrist*, of a poster showing the disembodied genitalia of men and women. The album cover featured a sticker warning that there was an enclosure "that some people may find shocking, repulsive, or offensive. Life can sometimes be that way." Although Biafra was acquitted, the suit led to the disbanding of the group and, according to Biafra, kept him from performing for more than a year.[15]

There is no doubt that groups like the Dead Kennedys are deliberately provocative in their lyrics and their performances, but outrageous behavior has been a hallmark of rock music from its very beginning. The attempts of adults to eliminate the raunchier aspects of the music are as foolish today as they were when cameramen were told to crop out the pulsating lower half of Elvis Presley's body when he appeared on *The Ed Sullivan Show*.

Tipper Gore and others claim that today's music is sometimes unacceptably offensive. By her standards Gore may be right, but no individual or group should be able to take the position of arbiter of what is available to others with less "refined" tastes. Our human tendency to attribute to the potential actions of "lesser" others what we fear in our own imaginations needs to be recognized and curtailed.

Meese and His Mission

With the rise of the New Right and the election of Ronald Reagan, the anti-obscenity forces looked forward to a new era of success. The administration did indeed develop strong links to the Moral Majority, the National Federation for Decency, and other organizations whose agenda included stamping out what they regard as smut. The antipornography issue seemed a natural ingredient for the federal government's efforts to restore "traditional values," which included shoring up the nuclear family. To this intent, people who were active in right-wing circles, including moral crusader Alfred Regnery, were appointed to key positions that enabled them to use taxpayer money to fund research and otherwise allocate funds for their own objectives.

Acting under pressure from "pro-decency" organizations, the administration in 1985 created a commission on pornography under the authority of Attorney General Edwin Meese. From the start, it was clear that the goal of the Meese Commission was to rebut the findings of the earlier National Commission on Pornography and its controversial 1970 report. The body was also expected to provide justification for expanded law enforcement and private campaigns against sexually explicit material. The bias of the Meese Commission was apparent in its list of appointees, which included nine known conservatives and several law enforcement officers. The Commission chair, Henry Hudson, was a Virginia district attorney who was well-known for his drives against pornography.

The Commission arranged public hearings in six cities, with emphasis placed on documenting the link between pornography and antisocial behavior. The hearings were carefully staged, with anonymous witnesses—claiming to be victims of pornography—often testifying from behind screens to protect their identities. Despite the potential impact of restrictions on literature and the arts, no attempt was made to invite testimony from writers, artists, or any of their organizations.[16] Whenever solicited testimony went against the dominant view of the Commission, it was simply rejected. According to Commission members Judith Becker and Ellen Levine, who entered a partial dissent to the final report:

> The paucity of certain types of testimony, including dissenting expert opinion, and the haste and absence of significant debate with which other recommendations and their supporting arguments were prepared did not leave adequate time for full and fair discussions of many of the more restrictive and controversial proposals.[17]

Moreover, several of the experts cited by the Commission to support its view of the link between pornography and antisocial behavior disputed the characterization of their research. Edward Donnerstein, a psychologist at the University of Wisconsin, denied that his research established causation, maintaining that his findings had consistently pointed to aggression, with and without sexual connotation, as the key problem. Donnerstein also criticized the Commission for limiting its focus to sexually explicit material:

> Males in our society have callous attitudes toward rape. But where do these come from? . . . We would be reluctant to place the blame on the media. If anything, the media act to reinforce already existing attitudes and values regarding women and violence. They are a contributor, but only one of many.[18]

Even before the Meese Commission issued its proposals, it took two actions that cast its integrity into question. Once it became clear that a great variety of groups that opposed the conduct of the hearings were closely monitoring its operations, the Commission tried—unsuccessfully—to prevent distribution of the transcripts of the hearings. Second, in February 1986 the Commission sent a letter to thousands of magazine retailers, including the 7-Eleven and Rite-Aid chains, informing them that an anonymous witness—who turned out to be the Reverend Donald Wildmon of the National Federation for Decency—had named them as distributors of pornography, and that this fact would be included in the Commission's final report unless they provided contrary information. Although a court ordered the Commission to send out a second letter retracting the earlier one, many stores, including the aforementioned chains, decided that it would be prudent to stop selling such magazines as *Playboy* and *Penthouse.*

When the work of the Meese Commission got started, attorney Barry Lynn of the American Civil Liberties Union declared that "a train was leaving the station marked censorship." This prophecy was confirmed a year later when the Commission's final report was released at a press conference held by Attorney General Meese (who, to the amusement of proponents and critics alike, found himself standing in front of a bare-breasted statue called *Spirit of Justice*).[19]

Despite its efforts to do so, the Commission was unable to produce proof to support the contention that pornographic materials inflict harm on society; it could assert only that certain kinds of especially violent material seem to have a pernicious effect. The Commission also allowed that it could not come up with a better definition of obscenity than the one contained in the Supreme Court's *Miller* decision.

This lack of supporting evidence did not stop the Commission from recommending that prosecutors use a number of laws originally enacted for non-speech-related purposes to curtail the activities of persons it deemed to be violating certain standards of decency. Among the actions it proposed were prosecuting pornographers for unfair labor practices, seizing the assets of companies involved in the smut business, and creating a federal database on those persons convicted for or suspected of activity related to obscenity.

The database proposal raised serious issues regarding invasion of privacy. Equally troubling was the Commission's encouragement that crusaders for morality ignore the First Amendment:

> Citizens should be aware of the legal criteria for distinguishing material which is obscene from that which is merely distasteful to some. However, citizen groups may wish to focus on materials which are not legally obscene and which are constitutionally protected from government regulation.

The Commission's report turned out to be a best-seller at government bookstores, though it appeared that many of the eager purchasers were interested not so much in its conclusions as in the 300-page section that included graphic descriptions of hundreds of "adult" magazines, books, and films.

The Aftermath

The Meese Commission report gave a green light to the efforts of local antipornography crusaders. Bills modeled after the Commission's recommendations have been introduced in numerous states. The Kansas legislature passed a law making retailers of pornography responsible for the content of what they sell. In Belgrade, Montana, a town of 3,200 with no "adult" bookstores, a committee was set up to ban such material in the event that it became necessary. Virginia passed a law, later modified by court challenges, making it a crime for bookstores to display sexually explicit material where it might be seen by minors.[20] The danger of allowing local officials to set standards was made frighteningly clear in 1987 when police in Orlando, Florida, nearly destroyed a Picasso print that was mixed in with confiscated pornographic material being thrown into an incinerator.[21]

At the federal level, Edwin Meese's Justice Department formed an Obscenity Enforcement Unit and announced that racketeering charges would be used to prosecute pornographers. The Reagan administration shrewdly placed its greatest emphasis on the suppression of child pornography—the aspect of the anti-obscenity effort that enjoys the most public support. Action in this area is based on a 1977 federal law as well as a 1982 Supreme Court ruling flatly denying First Amendment protection to portrayals of specifically described sexual acts by children under sixteen years of age.[22]

In September 1987 New York Newsday revealed that the U.S. Postal Service was running a "sting" operation to track down buyers as well as distributors of child pornography. The program, code-named Project Looking Glass, angered even some strong supporters of the crackdown on child pornography because of the entrapment involved in having postal inspectors solicit customers through a phony business front. More than one hundred alleged purchasers of child pornography were indicted in the scheme.[23]

The campaign against pornography in the electronic media has escalated as well. One major area of debate has been cable television. For a number of years heated debate has surrounded the ability of government authorities to regulate the erotic programming that became part of the fare as cable systems spread across the country in the 1970s. Cable operators did not like the controversy generated by offerings like the Playboy Channel, but they did covet the revenues such programming brought in, and to stay consistent with their resistance to the government control of rates, they had to come out against government censorship. Nonetheless, a number of states and localities passed restrictive legislation. The most aggressive was Utah, which enacted three laws, including one overruled by the Supreme Court in 1987 on First Amendment grounds.[24]

The Federal Communications Commission has also gotten into the act with a new policy aimed at suppressing "indecent" programming by television and radio broadcasters. Despite the FCC's dogged promotion of the deregulation of other aspects of broadcasting, it decided to take a more interventionist stance in this particular regard, noting that its 1987 decision was made in response to mounting public complaints about allegedly offensive radio talk shows.

The FCC's right to prohibit what it considered indecent (not to mention obscene) broadcasts was affirmed by the Supreme Court in 1978 in a case arising out of the airing of a comedy monologue by George Carlin called "Filthy Words" by listener-sponsored WBAI-FM in New York City. Although it prevailed in the WBAI case, the FCC's tendency in the following decade has been to limit its role to prohibiting the utterance on the air of the seven words it found objectionable and thus relegated as taboo in the Carlin routine.

That changed with the 1987 policy shift. The FCC indicated that it would once again apply a stricter interpretation of indecency during those hours that children were likely to be in the audience; at other times, defined as the period from midnight to six A.M., broadcasters were given more latitude, though even during this liberated time period viewers and listeners have to be warned when material termed offensive is about to be broadcast on their radio or television.

Despite the relatively safe harbor created for late-night programming, the FCC's new approach has sent a chill through the broadcasting world. In light of the uncertain climate, WBAI sought to get clearance from the FCC on the station's plan to air its annual reading of Joyce's *Ulysses*; the FCC declined to give an advance ruling. WBAI's parent organization, the Pacifica Foundation, decided it was too risky to broadcast a program featuring Allen Ginsberg reading his famous poem *Howl*. The Pacifica stations did air an interview with Ginsberg, in which he described the FCC's approach as "a mirror image of the Stalinist mentality."

Feminists and the Pornography Issue

As the antipornography movement gained new momentum in recent years, it created a great furor in the feminist community. Most feminists agreed that pornography, at least in some forms, contributed to the oppression of women. But the movement became deeply split on whether this fact justified joining with those activists, usually from quarters that were not sympathetic to the feminist cause, who called for restrictions on the production and sale of objectionable material.

Positions tended to be polarized because of the hard line taken in favor of suppressing pornography, by activists like Susan Brownmiller, Andrea Dworkin, and Catharine MacKinnon.

Brownmiller, the author of *Against Our Will: Men, Women and Rape*, condemned pornographic material for encouraging a cultural climate in which men feel it is their right to use violence against women. In 1981 she was a co-founder of Women Against Pornography, which organized to fight peep shows and other porn businesses in New York's Times Square area.

Dworkin, another leading feminist writer, and MacKinnon, a law professor, developed a legal strategy for attacking pornography as a violation of women's civil rights. They framed an antipornography ordinance that was adopted by the city council of Minneapolis but was vetoed by its mayor; a similar ordinance was then adopted in Indianapolis. The law was challenged, and in a strongly worded opinion, Federal Judge Sarah Barker declared it unconstitutional. She wrote:

> To deny free speech in order to engineer social change in the
> name of accomplishing a greater good for one sector of our

society erodes the freedoms of all and, as such, threatens tyranny and injustice for those subjected to the rule of such laws.

As the Indianapolis case moved to the Supreme Court, feminists who opposed censorship mobilized to try to discourage a ruling that could undermine free speech. They formed groups such as Women Against Censorship and the Feminist Anti-Censorship Task Force (FACT), which submitted a brief urging the Court to reject an approach that not only weakened constitutional principles but also portrayed women as weak, helpless members of society in need of special protection. In 1986 the justices upheld the lower court ruling without comment.[25]

Feminist opposition to the Dworkin/MacKinnon approach has not been limited to the legal issues. In publications such as *Caught Looking*, the anticensorship forces have also resisted what they see as the tendency of the pornography debate to ignore the erotic impulses of women.[26] Moreover, Betty Friedan and other writers have called the pornography issue a red herring that takes attention away from more pressing matters for women, such as domestic violence, child care, and poverty.

Sexual McCarthyism

The recent antipornography movement represents yet another attempt by certain groups to impose their morals on the rest of society. What makes these efforts more threatening than those of the past is the extent to which they have been abetted by federal, state, and local authorities. The climate engendered by initiatives such as the Meese Commission has been described with only a bit of hyperbole by Hugh Hefner as "sexual McCarthyism."[27]

Maintaining a strong defense against these drives for censorship is made more difficult by the alarmingly high level of sexual violence and abuse that continues to plague American society. But there is still no definitive evidence that sexually explicit materials contribute to the problem. Focusing on pornography amounts to attacking the symptoms rather than the disease itself, which is the actual subordination of women—a condition that many of the nonfeminist crusaders prefer not to address. In addition, zealous antipornography efforts end up targeting all erotic material, thus contributing to another form of sexual repression. With the exception of child pornography—where the participants in the production of the material are exploited against their will—there is no justification for allowing the state to decide what words and images we may or may not expose ourselves to. The spread of censorship is ultimately more offensive than any pornography.

Notes

1. John Cohen, ed., *The Essential Lenny Bruce* (New York: Ballantine Books, 1967), p. 288.

2. Brennan dissent, Roth v. U.S., 354 U.S. 476 (1957).

3. For more on Comstock, see Gay Talese, *Thy Neighbor's Wife* (New York: Dell, 1980), p. 65. Talese calls Comstock "the most awesome censor in the history of America."

4. See Barbara Ehrenreich's criticism of the Meese Commission report in Philip Nobile and Eric Nadler, *United States of America vs. SEX* (New York: Minotaur, 1986), p. 334.

5. In the Hicklin case, the Court said that the test of obscenity was "whether the tendency of the matter charged as obscenity is to deprave and corrupt those whose minds are open to such immoral influences, and into whose hands a publication of this sort may fall." This quotation is from the Brennan dissent in Paris Adult Theatre I. v. Slatoon, 413 U.S. 49 (1973).

6. But once in a while a decision went the other way, as in the case of Edmund Wilson's *Memoirs of Hecate County* (New York: Doubleday, 1946), in which the book was found obscene by the courts of New York. The Supreme Court split 4 to 4, with Judge Frankfurter abstaining because of his friendship with Wilson, thereby sustaining the conviction.

7. One exception to this trend involved the conviction of Ralph Ginzburg in 1966 for mailing erotic advertising. Here, the Court appeared to base its decision not on content but on evidence that Ginzburg was "pandering."

8. For more about the 1960s marriage of the underground press and mass-market erotica, see Laurence Leamer, *The Paper Revolutionaries* (New York: Simon and Schuster, 1972).

9. Congress in Public Law 90-100 assigned four specific tasks: "(1) *with the aid of leading constitutional law authorities,* to analyze the laws pertaining to the control of obscenity and pornography; and to evaluate and recommend definitions of obscenity and pornography; (2) to ascertain the methods employed in the distribution of obscene and pornographic materials and to explore the

nature and volume of traffic in such materials; (3) to study the effect of obscenity and pornography upon the public, and particularly minors, and its relationship to crime and other antisocial behavior; and (4) to recommend such legislative, administrative, or other advisable and appropriate action as the Commission deems necessary to regulate effectively the flow of such traffic, *without in any way interfering with constitutional rights*" (emphasis added).

10. *Report of the U.S. Commission on Obscenity and Pornography* (Washington, DC: GPO, September 1970).

11. The Miller test would determine 1. whether the "average person, applying contemporary community standards would find that the work, taken as a whole, appeals to the prurient interest; 2. whether the work depicts or describes in a patently offensive way, sexual conduct specifically defined by the applicable state law; and 3. whether the work, taken as a whole, lacks serious literary, artistic, political or scientific value."

12. "Is TV Sex Getting Bolder?" *TV Guide*, 8–14 August 1987, p. 2.

13. See Tipper Gore, *Raising PG Kids in an X-Rated Society*, (Nashville, TN: Abingdon, 1987).

14. "Record Companies Finesse PMRC," *Rolling Stone*, 8 May 1986. See also, Juliet L. Dee, "Media Accountability for Real Life Violence: A Case of Negligence or Free Speech," *Journal of Communication*, Spring 1987, p. 128.

15. "Singer's Trial on Nudity in Album Begins Today," *The New York Times*, 10 August 1987. See also Steven Wishnia, "Rockin' with the First Amendment," The *Nation*, 24 October 1987.

16. A group of artists joined with other critics of the Commission at a press conference organized by the National Coalition Against Censorship. Their statements are contained in *Meese Commission Exposed*, published by the NCAC (New York, 1986).

17. Attorney General's Commission on Pornography, *Final Report* (Washington, DC: GPO, 1986).

18. Edward Donnerstein and Daniel Linz, "Mass Media Sexual Violence and Male Viewers," *American Behavioral Scientist* 29, no. 5 (May/June 1986).

19. The ACLU published a fine summary and critique of the Commission's final report in "Polluting the Censorship Debate," *ACLU*, June 1986.

20. Virginia v. American Booksellers Association, 598 F.Supp. 1316 (S.D. Ind. 1984); affirmed, 771 F2d 323 (7th Cir. 1985). Affirmed by the Supreme Court in 1986 without a written opinion.

21. "Picasso Etching Saved from Fire," *The New York Times*, 1 August 1987.

22. New York v. Ferber, 458 U.S. 747 (1982).

23. "Nationwide Postal 'Sting' Snares Kiddie Porn Buyers," *New York Newsday*, 1 September 1987; "100 Indicted in Pornography Sting," *New York Newsday*, 15 September 1987.

24. "High Court Upholds Ruling Striking Down Utah Indecency Statute," *Broadcasting*, 30 March 1987.

25. American Booksellers Association v. Hudnut, 598 F.Supp. 1316 (S.D. Ind. 1984); affirmed 771 F.2d 323 (7th Cir. 1985); 54 U.S.L.W. 3560 (U.S. 24 February 1986).

26. Hannah Alderfer, Beth Jaker, and Marybeth Nelson, *Caught Looking: Feminism, Pornography and Censorship* (New York: Caught Looking, 1986).

27. Hugh Hefner, "Sexual McCarthyism," *Playboy*, January 1985, p. 58.

Selected Readings

Alderfer, Hannah, Beth Jaker, and Marybeth Nelson. *Caught Looking: Feminism, Pornography and Censorship*, New York: Caught Looking, 1986.

Daly, Mary. *GYN/Ecology*. Boston: Beacon Press, 1978.

Dworkin, Andrea. *Pornography*. New York: Putnam, 1981.

Gardner, Gerald. *The Censorship Papers: Movie Censorship Letters from the Hays Office 1934 to 1968*. Dodd, Mead, 1987.

MacKinnon, Catharine. *Feminism Unmodified*. Cambridge, MA: Harvard University Press, 1987.

Marsh, David. *Rock 'n' Roll Confidential*. New York: Pantheon, 1985.

National Coalition Against Censorship. *Meese Commission Exposed*. New York: NCAC, 1986.

Norwich, Kenneth. *Lobbying for Freedom: A Citizen's Guide for Fighting Censorship at the State Level*. New York: St. Martin's Press, 1975.

Talese, Gay. *Thy Neighbor's Wife*. New York: Dell, 1980.

5

BIG BROTHER AND
THE HOLDING COMPANY

Censorship Inside
the Corporation and the Media

If a modern-day Dante were to tour the American corporation, he would see written above the portals: "Abandon all individual rights, ye who enter here." To an alarming extent, the constitutional liberties that Americans take for granted are absent from the workplace.

More than eighty percent of nongovernmental workers have virtually no right to object to wrongful company action and may be discharged for criticizing their employers or for engaging in certain kinds of outside political activity. While some laws protect collective actions by workers, almost no statute exists to safeguard the speech, association, and privacy interests of individual employees. David Ewing, former editor of the *Harvard Business Review,* calls the absence of employee freedom in the private sector the "black hole of American rights." [1]

In the past decade, this situation has improved to a limited extent as laws have been passed to provide protection to employees who engage in whistleblowing to reveal improper or illegal acts by their employers. Yet the stakes here are still high. People who "blow the whistle" often lose their jobs and pensions and find themselves ostracized by their colleagues, who, while they may be sympathetic, fear to be associated with those who openly oppose management. Typically, whistleblowers find it difficult to obtain another position. Much remains to be done to provide legal protection for those who risk their livelihood to inform the public about corporate misconduct.

Corporate suppression of free speech is particularly problematic in the media and publishing industries. Here companies are both employers and purveyors of expression. The last section of this chapter will discuss instances in which, because of ideological reasons or external pressure, these corporations have altered or withdrawn works that were being written for them under contract.[2]

Masters and Servants: The History of Employer Control

The traditional relationship between employers and workers in the United States, as in most other countries, has been based on the master/servant model. Although the U.S. Constitution provided more rights to the working class than existed in other societies, these liberties were not extended to the workplace.

This is most clearly the case with regard to those principles embodied in the Bill of Rights. The First Amendment forbids only the government from interfering with free expression and association. Private entities have been exempt, unless they were so closely tied to government activities that their operations were considered a form of "state action."

As the country industrialized during the nineteenth century, small establishments in which the owners had close personal bonds with their employees were overtaken by larger, more impersonal corporations. The old traditions of employee loyalty and employer/master paternalism broke down and were replaced by a strictly economic relationship. Under this new system of wage labor, employers were free to hire and fire at will, and workers could sell their services wherever they chose. In theory, the two parties were equal participants in the labor market, but in practical terms workers had even less freedom than before. Employers enjoyed a position of dominance, and property rights were considered sacrosanct, especially by the courts. In a major ruling handed down in 1884, a Tennessee court ruled that employers "may dismiss their employees at will . . . for good cause, for no cause, or even for cause morally wrong, without being thereby guilty of legal wrong."[3]

In the early twentieth century, the Supreme Court came down squarely on the side of private power when it elevated the employer's absolute right to discharge his employee to a constitutionally protected right. In cases involving workers who were fired because of their membership in labor unions, the due process right of the employers was said to be violated by state laws that interfered with the right of the "purchaser of labor" to set conditions.[4]

Workers have long fought to establish free speech rights. In the early years of the century, the intrepid Industrial Workers of the World ("Wobblies") defied local laws forbidding them from holding open-air meetings. The Wobblies made this battle over their First Amendment rights the centerpiece of their radical organizing efforts.[5] By and large, the courts were unsympathetic.

The labor struggles of the 1930s produced legislation that established the right of workers to unionize. In contrast to the early blanket support for employer control, court decisions attempted to balance the competing rights of employers and labor. On one occasion, the Supreme Court held that the First Amendment guarantees of religious freedom applied to a company town.[6]

In another instance, the Court upheld the National Labor Relations Act's protection of employee speech but specified that this applied only to issues that were subject to collective bargaining.[7] Since that time, there has been a dichotomy between legally protected speech that is part of collective action and the unprotected speech of individual employees.[8]

After World War II, the giant corporations that had come to dominate the nation's economy developed organizational cultures that did even more to stifle individual expression. These vast bureaucracies fostered conformity and discouraged individual assertiveness. The regimented atmosphere further strengthened employer control by linking employee compliance to promotions, prosperity, and peer approval.

Only in the 1960s did the powerful rule of managerial prerogative begin to weaken. The first sign came when civil rights legislation, outlawing discrimination based on race, religion, or gender, was applied to private employers. At the same time, because of the closer ties that had been forged between the federal government and business, there was a growing sentiment for extending additional constitutional protections to private-sector employees. Writers like John Kenneth Galbraith began to point out that large corporations, especially those tied to the Pentagon and NASA, were essentially extensions of the government.

Others argued that large private entities, including labor unions, now had the power to threaten individual freedom seriously and should be subject to limited regulation to assure First Amendment liberties.[9] The colonialists, they contended, could not have imagined the immense power wielded by General Motors or AT&T. And no wonder: In the early 1960s, the Fortune 500 companies employed some four million people, exceeding the total population of the United States in the year 1790.

One of the nation's foremost First Amendment scholars, Thomas Emerson, wrote: "Many private centers of power are so related to the formal government that the requirement of 'state action' can be found to bring the First Amendment into play." How this could be done presented a complex and difficult issue, Emerson noted. Autonomous private entities helped limit the power of government. However, he observed, "a system of freedom of expression that allowed private bureaucracies to throttle all internal discussion of their affairs would be seriously deficient."[10]

By the early 1970s, several trends had emerged that have continued to extend the rights of private-sector employees. First, there was a growing public perception of the American corporation as a social as well as an economic entity, with consequent social responsibilities. In Washington, regulatory agencies such as OSHA and EPA were established to research and monitor corporate activities that affected the public welfare.

Galbraith's observations about the "new industrial state" were borne out as the economy became more reliant on the scientific and technological sectors, where the federal government was often a principal client. A move began in academic circles to "constitutionalize" the corporation.

While union membership was on a steep decline, individual employees became more assertive. They sought greater job satisfaction and participation in decision making, in addition to better hours and wages. Moreover, an increasingly better educated work force brought notions of fairness and equity into the workplace; the new perspective maintained that the employee's duty as a citizen transcends his duties as an employee. The issue of individual employee rights outside a union context took on new importance.

The First Amendment rights of corporations also were expanded significantly in the 1970s. After years in which these rights had been interpreted narrowly, the Supreme Court ruled that a large corporation had just as much right to participate in the political process as anyone else.[11] But should a "corporate person" enjoying almost full First Amendment rights of expression be required to abide by the same principles when its own employees spoke out on issues of public importance? That question was still to be decided.

"Dagwood, You're Fired!"—The Speech Rights of Employees

In 1968, the Supreme Court upheld the speech rights of public employees.[12] The central question was whether a schoolteacher had lost her constitutional right to free speech concerning a matter of public importance when she accepted public employment. The Court left no doubt that the answer was no. Following the reasoning in a landmark libel case a few years earlier,[13] it ruled that unless she had exhibited reckless disregard for the truth, her exercise of First Amendment rights could not be grounds for discharge.

The same rule has not been established for private-sector employees. Without proof that they are significantly involved in government work, the rights to free speech for these workers are not protected by the Constitution. The extent to which their speech is protected depends upon applicable federal and state laws, and on court determinations made on a case-by-case basis.

Unionized Employees

The rights of unionized workers are spelled out in a series of federal laws prohibiting employer interference in collective labor activity.[14] The protection for people covered by union contracts, though stronger than for the nonunionized, nongovernmental worker, is also incomplete.

For example, an employee engaged in union activity may still be punished for speech-related conduct if the information provided lies outside the narrow bounds of wages and working conditions. In 1987, American Airlines fired some two dozen flight attendants for distributing a brochure at the Dallas–Fort Worth airport on their own time. The brochure was part of a campaign by the Association of Professional Flight Attendants (APFA) to mobilize public support for the union's effort to eliminate a two-tier wage system. Entitled "American Airlines—Doing What They Do Best?" the brochure criticized the airline for giving its executives "six-figure" salaries while paying workers "poverty-level wages." It also cited airline management problems with safety violations, price fixing, and the dumping of toxic waste.

The airline reacted angrily to the leaflet distribution and discharged all those involved, basing its action on the claim that the employees had no right to distribute to third parties information disparaging their employer and "unrelated to ongoing negotiations." It took several months for a federal district court to rule that it did not have jurisdiction and to refer the case to the relevant federal agency. During that time, the dismissed flight attendants remained out of work. In August 1987, the flight attendants were rehired. American claimed it was doing the rehiring "as a matter of clemency," and that the distribution of similar material in the future would result in immediate discharge.[15]

The inclination of employers and the courts to clamp down on dissident speech by workers poses a serious challenge to the modern labor movement. Over the past decade many unions have realized that they could achieve their aims only if they went beyond the narrow confines of traditional collective bargaining. In order to take their case for economic justice to wider audiences, labor organizations (including APFA at American Airlines) have adopted such tactics as the corporate campaign, designed around their members' ability to speak out critically on management practices in order to attract public support. The moves by corporations like American Airlines to discourage this effort by firing workers and bringing lawsuits have a chilling effect on the attempts of unions to use free speech as a tool in labor relations.

Nonunionized Workers

Generally, the rights of free expression for those who work for nonunionized companies are in an even more vulnerable position than for workers covered by union contracts, who are guaranteed minimum due process of law through grievance and arbitration procedures. These nonunion workers are subjected to subtle, daily pressures to toe the line. As Dagwood knows, they can be fired at any moment.

Company practices in this area are extremely difficult to monitor. It may be impossible to prove that actions such as demotions and geographic transfers are a result of employee dissidence rather than a negative performance evaluation.

For the most part, harsh penalties still are imposed against employees who follow their conscience. It is standard throughout industry that, whatever openness is encouraged at the outset, once management has reached a decision everyone is expected to be part of the team. Too often, those who do not join in become nonpersons.

Whistleblowers: The Perils of Speaking Out

Some people do speak out. The term "whistleblowers" is used to refer to those individuals within corporations or government bureaucracies who go public with disclosures of improper activities on the part of their employers.

Whistleblowers have often been the only way that the public and government regulatory agencies have learned about dangerous products and threats to public health and safety. Many such citizens venture out on uncharted ground, refusing employer instructions to commit perjury, falsify financial documents, or cover up environmental violations that the company has knowingly committed.

Chuck Atchison, a quality control inspector for Brown & Root, was responsible for revealing safety violations in the nuclear power plant his employer was building near Glen Rose, Texas, for the Texas Utilities Electric Company. Karen Silkwood, it is said, paid with her life for trying to blow the whistle on lapses in safety at Kerr-McGee's plutonium processing plant in Cimarron, Oklahoma.

Historically, telling on the company was strictly taboo, running counter to well-established rules of employee loyalty and confidentiality. Attitudes toward whistleblowing began to change in the 1970s, particularly with the influence of consumer advocate Ralph Nader. In 1971, Nader organized a conference on the topic of whistleblowing that brought forth compelling testimony from those who had exposed corporate wrongs. During a period of almost continual revelations of unethical corporate and governmental conduct, Nader helped place whistleblowing on the agenda of public policy.[16]

Not long after this, the American Association for the Advancement of Science issued a report urging scientists and engineers to blow the whistle on their employers when they saw their work being used for morally dubious ends. Congress became involved in investigating the problems encountered by whistleblowers inside the government, which resulted in the Civil Service Reform Act of 1978.

Today many states have laws protecting public- and private-sector whistleblowers from retaliatory discharge. Yet these steps represent only incremental, partial reform. Penalties for whistleblowing, including demotion and ostracism, continue to discourage all but the most intrepid.

Whistleblowing becomes even more important at a time when companies are going to great lengths to ensure that their mistakes are not revealed. In September 1987, *The Wall Street Journal* reported that companies were shredding more internal documents than ever before.[17] A primary motive for this was to bury evidence that might be damaging in antitrust and product liability litigation. Ironically, the consultants being used to advise companies on destroying papers describe themselves as experts in "document retention."

The employee who calls attention to problems often believes that he or she is the person most loyal to the company. Roger Boisjoly of Morton Thiokol warned his superiors that the space shuttle *Challenger* might explode if launched under the weather conditions on the day of the launch. Interviewed on television months later, he said he believed he had acted in the best interest of the company's image and economic standing by expressing his opinion. After the explosion, he had hoped to be included in the project to redesign the booster; instead he found himself ostracized, and he soon resigned.

If one looks at what happens in the lives of most employees who go public with criticisms of their employers, it is clear that punishment is still the standard fate. Indeed, whistleblowers are persecuted heroes. Generally, they lose their jobs and then spend many months looking for new ones. Future employers regard what they have done as a stigma. In other words, much as things have changed during the last fifteen years, whistleblowing remains a risky activity indeed—a fact of which most employees are uncomfortably aware.

Laws Protecting Whistleblowers

Many people are aware that because of the antidiscrimination laws of the 1960s and 1970s, employers may no longer hire, fire, or promote people on the basis of race, sex, age, or religion. However, few know that Congress also has enacted numerous laws that protect employees who blow the whistle. Private-sector employees who make disclosures on issues of workplace health and safety are protected by more than a dozen federal laws. These laws cover workers in mining, nuclear power, and railroads, as well as in the broad regulatory arena of environmental safety. A recent addition covers employees of defense contractors who make, to members of Congress, the Department of Defense, and the Justice Department, disclosures "relating to a substantial violation of law related to a defense contract."[18]

In practice, these laws have had limited impact. Few people who make such revelations manage to retain their jobs. According to a recent report on the subject, one problem is that the laws "have created a crazy quilt of investigative, adjudicatory and review responsibilities."[19] This atmosphere of bureaucracy undermines any confidence that the existence of a law might provide to those contemplating disclosure of incriminating information. In addition to the flaws in such legislation, people in many sectors of the labor force have no legal protection at all in the circumstances described here. Fields in which new laws are needed include aviation and aeronautics, manufacturing, and the production of food, drugs, and other consumer goods.

Although the federal protection accorded whistleblowers declined during the 1980s, many states now provide protection for both government and private-sector workers where matters of public policy are involved. The adoption of such laws in recent years points to an important and perhaps historic change in the previously impenetrable domain of the private employer.

The first whistleblower statute, adopted by Michigan in 1980, followed an incident in which a chemical company mistakenly shipped a poisonous fire retardant to grain cooperatives and, as a result, many people were exposed to contaminated food. A company employee was asked to testify at a government inquiry but was told by his employer not to volunteer information to investigators. He spoke out nonetheless.

Michigan's law forbids employers to discharge, threaten, or otherwise discriminate against workers who report a suspected violation. Since this law was adopted, many states have enacted similar legislation.

Moreover, in 1983, Connecticut became the first state to pass a law more generally recognizing the speech rights of private-sector employees. This law allows workers to sue employers for discipline or discharge, claiming exercise of federal or state free-speech rights, so long as the disputed speech does not materially interfere with the person's on-the-job performance.

Despite the staunchly pro-management ideology dominant in Washington, the company whistleblower is gradually receiving more attention from lawmakers at the federal and local levels. The new legal protections are intended to establish the right of employees to request information from their employers about health and safety standards and to refuse unsafe and unhealthful work in certain circumstances. Some of the whistleblower statutes provide a cause of action against retaliatory discharge if the reasons for dismissal are contrary to public policy. The actual significance of the new protections is limited by various forms of on-the-job censure of those who break rank and by the continuing stigma against those who "squeal," which continues to make it extremely difficult for whistleblowers to find subsequent employment.

The Courts: Gains and Losses

The courts have also begun to limit employer actions that run contrary to public policy. In 1975, an employee was fired for agreeing to serve on a jury after her employer had written a letter asking that she be excused. Ruling in her favor, the court said that jury duty was too high on the scale of American institutions for employers to be allowed to behave in this fashion.

In 1983, a federal appeals court in Pennsylvania ruled that an insurance company worker had a right to refuse his employer's order that he lobby for reform of the state's no-fault insurance law. Courts have also strengthened employee rights by finding an implied duty of good faith on the part of employers and by ruling that promises made at the outset of an employment relationship are enforceable.

In a few instances, state courts have looked to the U.S. Constitution in extending the free speech rights of employees. A Texas court, for example, considering a case in which a hospital employee was fired for publishing an article critical of hospital care of the terminally ill, held that the public policy embedded in the First Amendment of the U.S. Constitution supported applying the Texas constitution to the private employment relationship.[20]

However, in hundreds of instances the employer has prevailed. In 1977, an Alabama court ruled for the employer when an employee was discharged for refusing to falsify medical records.[21] In 1982, a Texas court refused to permit a nursing home nurse's aid to sue when she was fired for complaining to her superiors about the poor care given patients. It seemed to make little difference that there was a Texas law requiring nursing home employees to report cases of neglect or abuse to the state licensing agency.[22] In a 1981 study by labor expert Alan Westin, it was found that employees discharged for exercising their rights to free expression were afforded only very inconsistent protection.[23]

"After Hours"—Employer Restrictions on Outside Political Activities

Private employers also have successfully penalized employees for expressing themselves on a range of nonworkplace matters. Employees have been dismissed, suspended, harassed, and denied promotions for advocating communism, homosexual rights, and feminism. They also have been punished for publishing articles or books that criticize their current or former employers and for taking public positions on controversial issues such as nuclear weapons and corporate investment in South Africa. In most instances the employer's action goes uncontested, and in cases that have reached the courthouse, employers have usually prevailed.

In the early 1980s, an employee of AT&T was fired after being arrested at a political rally he had attended on his own time. The court upheld the employer's action because it was persuaded that private employers had the authority to fire people on the basis of their political activities.

Ironically, companies have been restricting the free speech rights of their employees at a time when the courts have greatly strengthened the First Amendment rights of corporate entities. After decades of ruling that the speech rights of companies were significantly more limited than those of individuals, the courts have returned to the nineteenth-century notion that regarded corporations and individuals as being on an equal footing in the marketplace.

The ability of employers to interfere with the political activities of workers is potentially enhanced by new technological tools of management control. Many employers are now able to listen in on the personal telephone conversations or computer messages of their employees. Although companies claim that they do this only to check on productivity, it is all too easy for them to use information obtained through this monitoring for other purposes.

Burying Books: Censorship in the Communications Business

As conduits for the nation's culture, publishers and other media organizations are in a special position in relation to the Constitution. A primary tenet of the First Amendment is that citizens of a democracy should have access to diverse and competing information. In our society, privately owned entities have traditionally controlled what information reaches the public. Book publishers have been at the center of the nation's cultural and literary history. Radio and television are primary sources of political information and have become an important influence on the opinions of the American people.

At the same time, these gatekeepers of public knowledge are involved in a profitable business which in recent times has attracted larger corporations in search of diversifying their holdings. During the 1970s, conglomerate ownership in the book publishing world became the subject of controversy amid a merger wave that put giant companies such as Gulf + Western and ITT, with no prior experience in the book publishing world, in the position of being in charge of publishing decisions.

Some industry critics believe that the ascendancy of financial managers in the publishing business and the thirst for blockbuster profits have led to a narrowing of the range of information that most Americans are exposed to. Archibald MacLeish and Ben Bagdikian, among others, have argued that the search for the fast buck has done more than any official censorship could ever do to erode the base of public knowledge in America.

Is the marketplace of communications spurring censorship? To what extent has the bottom line become a handy rationale for decisions not to publish controversial material? Answers to these questions, while very important in assessing the free exchange of ideas, are beyond the scope of this investigation. What will be examined here are situations in which writers and artists under contract are pressured to make major changes in texts or have their works withdrawn as a result of outside pressure.

In one respect, the whole editorial process that exists in the print and broadcast media can appear to be a form of censorship. Since it is difficult to determine which of numerous reasons was the basis for a company's decision to alter content, there is no practical way in most instances of distinguishing between routine editorial selection and deliberate attempts to prevent certain ideas or information from being disseminated. Yet in certain particular instances, we can document publishers changing course midstream. That many such decisions are made in fear of massive libel suits that drain—or threaten to drain—a publisher's financial resources does not make these decisions less troubling.

• In 1972, the publisher Warner Modular Publications, was in the process of issuing a monograph by Noam Chomsky and Edward Herman entitled *Counter-Revolutionary Violence: Bloodbaths in Fact and Propaganda*. When executives of the parent company, Warner Communications, learned of the contents of the work, which accused the United States of engaging in terrorism in Vietnam and other countries, they were outraged. Distribution of the monograph was halted and advertising was canceled. Most of the copies printed were destroyed.

• In 1974, Prentice-Hall had scheduled a book that was expected to be a blockbuster. Gerald Zilg had spent five years investigating the powerful du Pont family and its vast holdings, which resulted in a 623-page work entitled *Du Pont: Behind the Nylon Curtain*. However, before the book was published, various du Ponts, concerned about the book's revelations, brought enormous pressure to bear on the publisher and on the Book-of-the-Month Club (which had named the book a Fortune Book Club selection). The publisher cut back the first printing, reduced the advertising budget by two-thirds and made no attempt to take advantage of the publicity generated by the du Pont family's opposition. Zilg sued du Pont and Prentice-Hall but eventually was defeated in court.

• In 1980, executives of the Washington Post Company succeeded in getting Harcourt Brace Jovanovich to pulp 20,000 copies of *Katharine the Great,* an unflattering biography of *Post* owner Katharine Graham, written by Deborah Davis. The book also included a less than glowing portrait of Graham's late husband. Although it was on its way to being a bestseller, publisher William Jovanovich responded to direct pressure from Graham and *Post* executive director Ben Bradlee by canceling its publication.

• In 1987, Macmillan canceled publication of a book on the Bingham family of Louisville by David Chandler, shortly before copies were scheduled to arrive in bookstores. Lawyers for the Bingham family, former owners of the *Louisville Courier-Journal* and *Louisville Times,* had obtained an advance copy of the work and had produced a legal memorandum five inches thick, challenging its contents. The part of the book that caused the most friction was the claim that Mary Lily Bingham, the source of the family's wealth, was allowed to become a morphine addict by her husband and doctor and was then allowed to die of neglect. Instead of pursuing the alternative of confirming accuracy or making appropriate changes, Macmillan decided to withdraw the work entirely. Chandler's book was later published by Crown.

Publishing companies jealously guard their First Amendment rights with regard to any government interference, but such examples show that they are hardly irreproachable when it comes to resisting outside pressure from powerful private institutions and individuals. Threats of libel suits and concerns that other powerful figures will find material embarrassing should not be acceptable pretexts for decisions not to publish information. The public needs to hold the Fourth Estate to its own assertions about the importance of an unfettered press that will disseminate information even when it is likely to cause discomfort or generate controversy. One of the chief arguments for a free press in America rests on the assumption that only when they are unrestrained can writers and publishers inform and enlighten the public they serve. The importance of this notion for a democratic society cannot be underestimated. Otherwise, censorship in communications will become entrenched by a publishing industry that has weakened its own awareness as well as that of the public.

Notes

1. David W. Ewing, *Freedom Inside the Organization.* (New York: Dutton, 1977).

2. Censorship pressures in the publishing world are addressed also in the chapters on book banning, the pornography debate, and libel.

3. Payne v. Western & A.R.R., 81 Tenn. 507, 518, (1884).

4. Adair v. United States, 208 U.S. 161 (1908); Coppage v. Kansas, 236 U.S. 1 (1915).

5. Philip S. Foner, *History of the Labor Movement in the United States: Vol. 4. The Industrial Workers of the World 1905–1917,* (New York: International Publishers, 1980), chaps., 7 and 8.

6. Marsh v. Alabama, 326 U.S. 501, 504–510 (1946).

7. NLRB v. Jones & Laughlin Steel Corp., 301 U.S. 45–46 (1937).

8. Twenty years after the Marsh case, the Court reversed a trespass conviction of members of a labor union who were arrested for picketing on the grounds of a shopping plaza (Amalgamated Food Employees Union v. Logan Valley Plaza, 1968). No similar protection has been accorded individuals acting apart from organized labor.

9. One of the pioneering discussions of this issue can be found in Lawrence E. Blades, "Employment at Will vs. Individual Freedom: On Limiting the Abusive Exercise of Employer Power," *Columbia Law Review* 67, no. 1404 (1967).

10. Thomas I. Emerson, *The System of Freedom of Expression* (New York: Vintage, 1970), pp. 676–677.

11. First National Bank v. Bellotti, 435 U.S. 765 (1978). This case overturned a Massachusetts law restricting use of corporate funds to influence the outcome of a state referendum.

12. Pickering v. Board of Education, 391 U.S. 563 (1968).

13. The New York Times v. Sullivan, 376 U.S. 254 (1964).

14. The National Labor Relations Act, 29 U.S.C. sec. 157, sec. 7, provides that "employees shall have the right to self-organization, to form, join or assist labor organizations, to bargain collectively through representatives of their own choosing, and to engage in other concerted activities for the purpose of collective bargaining or other

mutual aid or protection, and shall also have the right to refrain from any or all such activities except to the extent that such right may be affected by an agreement requiring membership in a labor organization as a condition of employment as authorized in Sect. 8(a)(3)."

15. "American Airlines Rehires Attendants It Fired During Negotiations," *The Wall Street Journal, 25 August 1987.*

16. The work of the conference was published as R. Nader, P. Petkas, and K. Blackwell *Whistleblowing 1. Report of the Conference on Professional Responsibility* (Washington, DC: 1972).

17. "U.S. Companies Pay Increasing Attention to Destroying Files," *The Wall Street Journal,* 2 September 1987.

18. Pub. L. No. 99-661, sec. 942(a)(1), adding 10 U.S.C. sec. 2409(a).

19. Report to the Administrative Conference of the United States, Eugene R. Fidell, *Federal Protection of Private Sector Health and Safety Whistleblowers* (Washington, DC: 1987).

20. Jones v. Memorial Hospital System, 677 S.W.2d 221 (Tex. Ct. App. 1984).

21. Hinrichs v. Tranquilaire Hospital, 325 So.2d 1130 (Ala. 1977).

22. Maus v. National Living Centers, Inc., 633 S.W. 2d 674 (Tex. Ct. App 1982) discussed in Marcia J. Staff and Charles Foster, Marcia J. Staff and Charles Foster, "Current Issues Affecting the Private Employee's Right to Freedom of Expression," *American Business Law Journal 23* (Summer 1985).

23. Alan F. Westin, *Whistleblowing!: Loyalty and Dissent in the Corporation* (New York: McGraw-Hill, 1981); Alan Westin and Stephan Salisbury, eds., *Individual Rights in the Corporation* (New York: Pantheon, 1980).

Selected Readings

American Civil Liberties Union. *The Rights of Employees.* New York: Bantam, 1983.

Bagdikian, Ben H. *The Media Monopoly.* Boston: Beacon, 1983.

Ewing, David W. *"Do It My Way or You're Fired!"* New York: Wiley, 1983.

Ewing, David W. *Freedom Inside the Organization.* New York: Dutton, 1977.

Kohn, Stephen. *Protecting Environmental and Nuclear Whistleblowers: A Litigation Manual.* Washington, DC: Nuclear Information and Resource Service, 1985.

Miller, Arthur S. *The Modern Corporate State.* Greenwich, CT: Greenwood, 1976.

Smith, Robert Ellis. *Workrights.* New York: Dutton, 1983.

Westin, Alan, and Stephan Salisbury, eds. *Individual Rights in the Corporation.* New York: Pantheon, 1980.

6
STRANGERS IN THE NIGHT
Government Surveillance and Harassment

Their convictions grew out of their good-faith belief that their actions were necessary to preserve the security interests of our country. The record demonstrates that they acted not with criminal intent, but in the belief that they had grants of authority reaching to the highest levels of government.

—From an April 1981 statement by President Ronald Reagan pardoning two former FBI officials who had been found guilty of authorizing illegal break-ins at the homes of antiwar activists in the early 1970s

Reagan's pardon of former FBI officials W. Mark Felt and Edward Miller did not represent, as some Americans thought at the time, an attempt to put an end to a shameful chapter in our history in which the civil liberties of dissidents were widely abused. Instead, the action was a signal to the country's police agencies that they could continue to conduct illegal activities against those who dared to disagree with and work against government policies. Certainly Mark Felt was responding to this message when he said, upon learning of the pardon: "This is going to be the biggest shot in the arm of the intelligence community for a long time."

After 1981, the Reagan administration made good on its implicit promise: The domestic surveillance of dissident groups and individuals expanded dramatically. Organizations involved with issues ranging from policy on Central America to the control of nuclear weapons have been subjected to a barrage of wiretaps, burglaries, infiltration, tax audits, and other forms of surveillance and harassment. A lawsuit to force the FBI to divulge documents under the Freedom of Information Act revealed that the Bureau had gathered some 4,000 pages of information on one group alone, the Committee in Support of the People of El Salvador (CISPES).

During this period, the traditional intelligence-gathering methods of the FBI and other agencies have been supplemented with two additional sources: massive computer databases and private surveillance groups. The automation and privatization of elements of government surveillance may be in keeping with the spirit of the present day, but they also serve to further entrench the dangers presented by old-fashioned spying: an erosion of free speech and of the right to disagree with the government. As in the past, a vaunted concern for protecting national security has, in the end, contributed to a narrowing of constitutional rights.

From Pinkertons to G-Men

Many elements of modern American domestic surveillance by the government arose from nineteenth-century employer practices that were developed to control organized labor. After the Civil War, business associations were formed in most industrial communities to thwart the growth of the emerging trade union movement. The associations took pains to brand labor organizers as subversives, and in this way they justified the hiring of private security guards to supplement local police forces. These guards, many of whom came from the Pinkerton Agency, came to be known as Pinkertons. They spied on the activities of workers and provoked violence, thus precipitating local police to make arrests and otherwise serve management interests in seeking to control unions.

In one infamous case of the 1860s, a group of coal operators in eastern Pennsylvania hired armed vigilantes who committed acts of violence, including murder, that were then attributed to a secret society of miners called the Molly Maguires, a name taken from an underground organization that existed in Ireland. Two dozen workers were charged with the crimes, and on the basis of false testimony from Pinkerton spies the miners were convicted. Ten of the twenty-four were hanged, and the rest were jailed. Only years later did historians determine that the alleged Pennsylvania Molly Maguires never existed but were only a fiction created to identify labor leaders as savage saboteurs.[1]

Over the following decades, many sectors of American industry continued to use private detectives and spies against labor organizers, with special efforts made against radicals like the members of the Industrial Workers of the World. Henry Ford created his own "Service Department," which compiled dossiers on individual employees and used strong-arm tactics to fight unionization. Business leaders also pushed for the expansion of public law enforcement agencies, which adopted many of the same repressive practices. According to one observer of the 1930s, local police in industrial areas became known as "American Cossacks" because of the activities they conducted against labor activists and radicals.[2]

By the early years of the twentieth century the drive to expand police functions extended to the federal government. In 1908 a Bureau of Investigation (BOI) was created within the Department of Justice. Since criminal investigations were considered the province of local authorities, the BOI's responsibilities until World War I were confined largely to enforcing federal laws regarding treason and interstate commerce. Congress was reluctant to create a national police force, partly out of respect for the doctrine of states' rights, but there was increasing pressure from a variety of groups and individuals who wanted the federal government to crack down on what they considered immoral behavior. Among the most prominent of these moral militants was Anthony Comstock, the leader of the crusade against pornography (see chapter 4).

Attitudes in Congress and the executive branch changed with the advent of World War I and the Russian Revolution. The tumult abroad provoked extreme fears about enemy spies and domestic radicals, which provided an opportunity for the Department of Justice to expand its intelligence activities.

In the history of national police operations, the importance of the 1919 appointment of J. Edgar Hoover to be chief of a new General Intelligence Division within the Department of Justice cannot be overestimated. One of Hoover's first activities was to promote the postwar "Red Scare" by compiling dossiers on individuals and political groups and issuing sensationalized charges to the press. He also helped organize the infamous Palmer Raids (named after Attorney General A. Mitchell Palmer), which involved rounding up thousands of supposed subversives, many of whom, including the noted anarchist Emma Goldman, were deported.

In 1924 Hoover was named director of the BOI, which became the Federal Bureau of Investigation. Congress has never passed a law specifying the FBI's mandate in the areas of surveillance and intelligence. The lack of such a defined field of responsibility gave Hoover extraordinary latitude in defining Bureau powers by shrewdly picking and choosing from among various presidential orders and directives.

The first of the directives Hoover pursued was signed by President Franklin Roosevelt in 1939, instructing the FBI to take charge of investigative work relating to "espionage, sabotage and violations of the neutrality regulations." The directive also requested local police departments to turn over to the FBI any information they collected on these matters. From then on, Hoover, who remained head of the FBI until his death in 1972, saw it as his personal mission to monitor the activities of anyone who, in his own vivid imagination, could be regarded as subversive.

After World War II, the Bureau's stature was greatly enhanced amid the new Red Scare. The FBI devoted vast resources to monitoring the activities of the Communist Party, those it identified as communist front organizations, and every individual it suspected of being sympathetic to the party's goals. Indeed, it is said that Hoover had so many informers in the organization that at times his own people may have constituted half the membership. Having swelled the ranks of the Communist Party and having stoked the fear of subversion, Hoover could confidently lobby Congress for additional funds to fight the allegedly expanding internal Red Menace.

FBI surveillance went far beyond targeting those who could in any sense be considered subversive. Recently released FBI records reveal that for decades the Bureau monitored the activities of dozens of prominent American writers, including Pearl Buck, Edna St. Vincent Millay, John Dos Passos, and James Baldwin.[3] Liberal academics were also spied on. College professor Penn Kimball, a victim of this surveillance, decided to take on the Bureau and, after a long battle, achieved an extraordinary victory in 1987 when the government publicly cleared his name.[4]

Other government agencies were also involved in domestic surveillance, including the Internal Revenue Service, the Immigration and Naturalization Service, the Treasury Department, and the Central Intelligence Agency, which by statute was allowed to operate only abroad. The CIA nevertheless ran a domestic mail-opening program from 1952 to 1973 without the knowledge of presidents Eisenhower, Kennedy, and Johnson. In 1952 the National Security Agency was created with the official aim of gathering foreign intelligence (like the CIA); this ultrasecret agency has also directed its efforts against domestic targets.

Partly because they emerged from the elite spy services of World War II, the NSA and the CIA have been allowed to operate with little supervision. Even presidents have been kept uninformed of their activities on the grounds that they did not have a "need to know" key elements of agency operations. Containing the information about intelligence activities to a narrow few also has served to contain accountability for illegal actions; if they are discovered, it is easy to dismiss those said to be in charge while their superiors can maintain their innocence. A loose chain of command has continued to facilitate covert operations that at times went far beyond what was legally authorized.

COINTELPRO and CHAOS

In 1956, the FBI launched a new initiative called COIN-TELPRO (short for "Counterintelligence Program") that represented a shift from simple surveillance to more aggressive infiltration and disruption of dissident organizations.

The initial target of COINTELPRO was the American Communist Party. The approach of the Bureau was exemplified in its actions against William Albertson, a top party official. Using what was known as the "snitch jacket" technique, the Bureau planted a document that made it appear that Albertson was a government informer. When the document was discovered, Albertson insisted that he had been framed; nonetheless, in an episode that heightened suspicion and caused turmoil among its other officials, he was expelled from the party. It was only years later that evidence emerged suggesting an FBI fabrication.[5]

As other protest movements arose in the 1960s, the FBI extended its COINTELPRO operations against hundreds of civil rights, antiwar, and New Left organizations. Considerably less attention was devoted to the activities of the far right.

Especially violent were the Bureau programs aimed at the Black Panther Party, at Puerto Rican independence activists, at the American Indian Movement, and at other militant groups among people of color. Among other techniques, anonymous-letter campaigns were used in the hope of turning movement leaders against one another and generally discouraging public support for their causes. In several known instances, FBI infiltrators conspired in the murder of movement leaders. Among these was Black Panther Fred Hampton, who was killed in bed during a 1969 raid by Chicago police. The officers had been given a floor plan of Hampton's apartment drawn by an FBI infiltrator who had become head of Black Panther security.

During this time, the CIA was also extensively involved in trying to undermine the growing protest movements in the United States. Its Operation CHAOS was established at the behest of the Johnson administration to determine if the antiwar movement was being influenced by foreign interests. The agency also provided intelligence to local law enforcement agencies and arranged to have its own operatives infiltrate and disrupt various radical organizations. Similar activities were being carried out by various intelligence entities within the military[6] and the state police.[7]

Another victim of FBI and CIA activities was the underground press, that diverse assortment of publications that expressed and empowered many of the social movements of the 1960s. Intelligence agents collected information on each paper's publisher, its sources of funds, and its staff members. Many underground newspapers were put out of business when they were abandoned by advertisers who had been pressured by the FBI. The Bureau also created obstacles to distribution, fomented staff feuds, and spread false information to create suspicion and confusion.[8]

To muddle things even more, the FBI sponsored its own "underground" publications to help gather intelligence and to further the spread of disinformation. The CIA funded the College Press Service, a Denver-based news organization, which had infiltrators on staff.[9] Harassment by the IRS, the Federal Communications Commission, and local police forces also helped bring about the demise of underground media.

Revelations and Reforms

During the time that government agencies were carrying out their "dirty tricks"—as such covert activities are referred to in intelligence parlance—most Americans, including the subjects of the surveillance, did not realize what was happening. Troubling incidents were interpreted as the consequence of disorganization, and many activists who suggested the possibility of extensive government interference were accused of being divisive and even paranoid.

A series of shocking revelations during the 1970s provided evidence of a widespread pattern of aggressive, often violent, interference by federal agents in legitimate political activities. During the course of several investigations, it became clear that the intelligence agencies had become a law unto themselves. For the first time in the nation's history, Congress was forced to take a serious look at the practices and the results of unbridled surveillance.

Investigations by a Senate committee chaired by Senator Frank Church revealed that thousands of law-abiding citizens who were suspected of no crime had been the victims of government harassment, warrantless wiretaps, illegal break-ins, and other official misconduct. The Church Committee concluded that:

> Domestic intelligence has threatened and undermined the constitutional rights of Americans to free speech, association and privacy. It has done so primarily because the constitutional system for checking abuse of power has not been applied.

From a broader perspective, the government's intelligence operations in the 1960s can be seen as having interfered with the course of history. The social movements that arose during the period, which sought to make fundamental changes in American society, were not allowed to develop naturally; instead, many either died prematurely or were subverted by infiltrators and provocateurs whose corrupting influence succeeded in discrediting them in the eyes of the public. As a consequence, it is impossible to know in what direction these movements might have gone or what they might have achieved without secret government intervention.[10]

One consequence of the disclosures was a call for measures to rein in the intelligence agencies. In 1976, Attorney General Edward Levi issued guidelines for domestic security operations that permitted full investigation of political groups only if specific evidence showed that the subjects were or were likely to be breaking federal laws through violent means. In another attempt to protect the rights of individuals, Congress passed the Foreign Intelligence Surveillance Act in 1978. This law created a court to rule on agency plans to conduct electronic surveillance of persons believed to be agents of foreign powers. It specified that judges were to balance the constitutional rights of Americans against the requests of intelligence agencies.[11]

While these changes did not outlaw domestic surveillance or even seriously limit the conduct of the intelligence agencies, they did promote a greater degree of restraint. During the Carter administration, several grand jury probes were launched into FBI misconduct, including the one that led to the conviction of Bureau officials Mark Felt and Edward Miller.

Surveillance Back in Fashion

As Ronald Reagan took office in 1981, conservative forces were clamoring for liberalization of the Levi guidelines and loosening of other surveillance restrictions. The Heritage Foundation, the conservative group that drew up an agenda for the new administration, maintained that the country was once again facing a threat of subversion and argued that intelligence agencies should be given a freer hand in pursuing investigations. President Reagan, who had himself cooperated with the FBI as an informer in the late 1940s,[12] concurred.

In December 1981, the president issued Executive Order 12333 on intelligence, which for the first time authorized the CIA to conduct domestic operations. The order stated that domestic intelligence-gathering did not have to be linked to a criminal investigation, thereby removing the need to observe constitutional and statutory procedures. So long as a person or group could be put under the heading of "foreign intelligence," "counterintelligence," or "terrorism," the CIA as well as the FBI could engage in spying, infiltration, and more disruptive tactics. Within a short time, the Justice Department issued new guidelines, relating the requirements under which the FBI could launch full-scale investigations of dissident groups. The Justice Department also claimed the power to authorize physical searches without court approval.

The tone of intelligence work for the duration of the Reagan administration had now been set. Soon, the FBI embarked on a campaign of close surveillance of groups opposed to U.S. policies in Central America, focusing on CISPES.[13] By the mid-1980s there was growing evidence of renewed FBI mail tampering and break-ins, and an unusually large number of IRS tax audits of political activists were in progress.

As they had during earlier surveillance of dissident groups, FBI agents began paying regular visits to the workplaces and homes of individuals engaged in protesting administration policies in Central America. Customs agents detained U.S. citizens returning from Nicaragua, interrogated them, made photocopies of their personal written materials, and turned them over to the FBI.[14] Dozens of burglaries occurred at the offices of groups engaged in working against Reagan administration foreign policies. Many activists familiar with similar operations over the last twenty years—some of whom had won damages from the government for illegal FBI wiretapping and burglaries—believe the recent break-ins were caused by FBI agents or by private organizations working with the FBI.

In response to these developments, the Center for Constitutional Rights in New York set up the Movement Support Network to act as a clearinghouse for reports of surveillance and harassment. By the end of 1987 it had assembled a 48-page compilation of such reported incidents over the previous four years.[15]

The nature and quantity of these incidents indicate a resurgence of FBI tactics reminiscent of COINTELPRO: the infiltration and disruption of dissident groups. In one example, Frank Varelli, an FBI operative who infiltrated the Dallas branch of CISPES in 1981 under a false name and remained active in the organization until 1984, later left the Bureau and went public with his story. He reported that his work for the Bureau included stealing documents and preparing false literature that was then distributed under the CISPES name. He also described having been instructed to develop a sexual relationship with one of the CISPES leaders in order to compromise her.[16] Moreover, Varelli said he served as a contact between the FBI and the Salvadoran National Guard, a contention that has strengthened already existing reports that the Bureau had been cooperating for some time with the murderous Salvadoran security forces.

Despite the revelations of the 1970s and the mounting evidence of a new campaign of government harassment of dissident groups, the mainstream media have tended to downplay the subject.[17] A turning point came in 1988 as the result of a lawsuit that had been filed by the Center for Constitutional Rights on behalf of CISPES, as part of an effort to obtain FBI documents under the Freedom of Information Act. After an eighteen-month legal battle, the Bureau agreed to release about 1,300 of the nearly 4,000 pages of material it said it had assembled on CISPES.

Although extensive parts of the released pages were blacked out, the materials provided ample evidence that the FBI had been conducting a massive campaign of surveillance against CISPES —which it had designated a potential "foreign terrorist" organization that could as a consequence be subject to the procedures outlined in Executive Order 12333—as well as against hundreds of other activist groups, including the Maryknoll Sisters, the United Church of Christ, and the United Automobile Workers. The FBI's techniques included inserting undercover agents in the groups, photographing peaceful demonstrations, compiling the names of people who wrote articles for student newspapers and spoke on radio talk shows, and recording the license-plate numbers of cars parked near demonstrations and conferences that related to protecting U.S. Central America policy.

The revelations made in January 1988 were so shocking that President Reagan publicly expressed his "concern" and asked for a review of the surveillance program. FBI Director William Sessions acknowledged that field agents had sometimes gone beyond their orders, but he defended the legitimacy of the program, which was said to have been initiated by his predecessor, William Webster, because of reports that CISPES had links to terrorist activity in Central America. White House spokesman Marlin Fitzwater then said the president was satisfied that the FBI program "had a solid basis for its initiation and continuation."

Not everyone inside the federal government felt that way. One of the Bureau's own agents found the FBI's surveillance of nonviolent opponents of the administration's Central America policy so repugnant that he refused in 1986 to carry out a Bureau investigation of peace groups in Illinois to search for evidence of supposed terrorist activities. In another case, John Ryan, a twenty-one-year veteran of the FBI, believed that the inquiry was an attempt to discredit people who were engaged in legitimate political dissent. According to Ryan, the price he paid for acting on his convictions was being fired in September 1987, when he was less than a year away from qualifying for his pension.[18]

Managing Political Emergencies

In addition to targeting current political activities, the Reagan administration concocted more drastic plans for the future. One of the main vehicles for this effort was the Federal Emergency Management Agency, a little-known government body that was created in 1979 to coordinate federal emergency assistance during earthquakes, floods, and other natural disasters. FEMA's mandate now has been extended to embrace what those in power consider another kind of national emergency: widespread political protest.

The principal figure in FEMA's transformation was its head, Louis Giuffrida, who served as a general in the California National Guard in the days of President Reagan's governorship there. During that time, Giuffrida worked closely with Edwin Meese to create a statewide network of military police who were prepared to be used against student radicals. During his tenure at FEMA, the agency was equipped with powerful computers that were compatible with those of the CIA, the NSA, and other intelligence agencies. FEMA also began providing training for local police officers, which included courses, some classified, such as "Planning for and Dealing with the Consequences of Terrorism in the Local Community."

According to newspaper reports based on information disclosed during the Iran-contra investigations, Lieutenant Colonel Oliver North worked with Giuffrida to draft plans that would have provided for the establishment of martial law in the event of large-scale protest such as might occur if the United States invaded Nicaragua. The plan, which envisioned the suspension of civil liberties, reportedly designated FEMA as the agency to be in charge in such a situation.[19]

Constitutional freedoms would also be abrogated by a scenario prepared by the Immigration and Naturalization Service. In a 1986 report entitled "Alien Terrorists and Undesirables: A Contingency Plan," said by its INS authors to be the result of a three-year investigation they conducted of Palestinian communities in thirteen American cities, the agency outlined several strategies that it claimed could be useful in times of (unspecified) national emergencies. In one scenario, new detention sites would be identified by the military for the imprisonment of persons of targeted nationalities. Executive orders and regulations would be issued in order to suspend constitutional provisions that require

82

warrants for the government's seizure of property and the making of arrests. The INS report also noted the importance of avoiding all rule-making procedures and of excluding the public from deliberations "on the basis of national security."[20]

During the Reagan era we also witnessed renewed emphasis on collaboration between federal intelligence agencies and local police forces—a relationship that, once again, has been justified largely on the basis of fighting alleged terrorism. For example, in October 1987 it was reported that the FBI and local police departments were expanding their foreign counterintelligence operations as a result of suspicions that Libyan and Iranian terrorists were planning offensives in the United States.

Drawing attention to purported foreign enemies as a pretext to expand operations against domestic targets has a long tradition. Police forces in many American cities have extensive histories of harassing local political activists. Major lawsuits against "Red Squads" in several localities have resulted in court decisions that impose restrictions on these police activities.

These legal pressures appear to have caused local police to be somewhat more cautious in their surveillance activities, yet there is evidence that they have not abandoned their former practices. Philadelphia police, for example, were assigned to special intelligence units that monitored political organizations in order to gather information on "potential terrorism" during the celebrations surrounding the bicentennial of the Constitution.[21] And in 1987, the New York City Police Department revealed that it was monitoring broadcasts of black-oriented radio station WLIB. Later that year the department revealed that undercover officers had improperly attended several meetings of the New York City Civil Rights Coalition.[22]

Private Spies

In keeping with the Reagan administration's emphasis on private initiative, the number and the resources of private groups that collect information about individuals whose political views differ from their own expanded significantly during the 1980s. These organizations vary in their objectives and strategies, but they are alike in their ability to function outside the legal constraints placed on government agencies. Several maintain close ties to members of the intelligence community as well as to some members of Congress.

Groups such as the Freedom Institute, the American Security Council, and the American Legion have assembled some of the nation's most elaborate computerized databases about millions of people. Like the FBI under J. Edgar Hoover, these groups use their information to create the image of a national political menace that justifies surveillance.

One of the most notorious of these private organizations is the Western Goals Foundation, which, during the Tower Commission investigations surfaced as one of Oliver North's main private contra support groups. Its principals have included late Congressman Larry McDonald, anticommunist impresario General John Singlaub, and right-wing fund-raiser Carl ("Spitz") Channell.[23]

In 1984, the American Civil Liberties Union brought a suit against Western Goals, charging that the organization had illegally obtained intelligence files maintained by the Los Angeles Police Department. Brought on behalf of fifteen organizations and thirty-seven individuals, including Joan Baez, Jackson Browne, and Norman Lear, the suit alleged that high-level police officials had authorized a detective to give Western Goals computerized access to the information. This suit was settled for $1.8 million.[24]

An investigation in 1987 by reporter Sylvia Chase of San Francisco's KRON-TV found that the Young America's Foundation, the Capital Research Center, and the Institute for Contemporary Studies were gathering intelligence on dissident groups and individuals by such methods as rummaging through the trash of target groups to obtain membership lists and other data.[25] Leaders of this self-described "commie-watching network" boasted that their efforts were endorsed by the Reagan administration and that their reports were used by the FBI and the Justice Department.

Another indication of close collaboration between government and private political entities is the case of a group called Americans for Human Rights and Social Justice. Phil Mabry, head of the organization, told the *Dallas Morning News* in 1987 that Oliver North had asked him in 1985 to spy on critics of the administration's Central America policies. Mabry enlisted volunteers to attend meetings and collect information on the Dallas–Fort Worth chapter of CISPES and the Inter-Religious Task Force on Central America.[26]

Monitoring the Monitors

Those wishing to track the activities of federal intelligence agencies must overcome multiple hurdles. If the efforts of the 1970s succeeded in curbing some government intelligence abuses, one of the major consequences of that restraint has been in the intensified efforts of intelligence agencies to stop the disclosure of information about their activities. The White House, Congress, and the courts have also helped to shield the intelligence community. Accountability is an even greater problem in regard to the agencies' use of private organizations that are not covered by disclosure laws.

The main statute providing public access to information about government programs is the Freedom of Information Act. Disclosures required by FOIA requests during the 1970s have been responsible for providing us with some of the most important information we have regarding agency misconduct. In one case alone, the tireless efforts of the Socialist Workers Party and its attorneys, as the FBI time and again denied FOIA requests for information, eventually produced evidence that led to a court ruling confirming that over a forty-year period the FBI had employed every imaginable tool of harassment to try to destroy the organization.

A 1982 presidential order that broadened agency authority to classify and thus withhold material has made it easier for the CIA and the FBI to conceal certain types of information. Congress has further limited public scrutiny by creating a new FOIA exemption for the operational records of the CIA and by broadening the exemption for criminal investigations so that it now encompasses any information compiled for law enforcement purposes. This same FOIA amendment permits agencies to deny the very existence of information they have gathered if it pertains to "foreign intelligence" or other programs that have been classified.

In 1985 a Supreme Court decision provided the agencies with another category for nondisclosure by expanding the scope of an FOIA exemption for an "intelligence source." In upholding the CIA's refusal to disclose the names of the institutions and individuals who participated in the the agency's MKULTRA experiment with brainwashing techniques, the Court said the exemption included anyone who might indirectly enable an observer to discover the identity of a CIA source.[27] A further shield for the CIA is a law making it a crime to disclose the names of intelligence agents (more on this in chapter 9).

The difficulty of employing the Freedom of Information Act to obtain information in the 1980s is exemplified by the experience of several peace groups housed in the basement of the Old Cambridge Baptist Church in Cambridge, Massachusetts. From November 1984 to June 1986, their offices were broken into eight times. (A week before the first break-in, the church had become a sanctuary for Central American refugees.) The groups strongly suspected that they were victims of illegal government action. They filed FOIA requests and discovered that all of the organizations were mentioned in FBI files. However, the Bureau withheld the relevant documents, either asserting a "national security" exemption or claiming that disclosure might reveal the identities of informers.

"Intelligence" by Bits and Bytes

Soon after he joined the Justice Department in 1919, J. Edgar Hoover started the first national "crime" index. It included the names and locations of "radically inclined" individuals, their organizations, and publications. Quickly expanded to include several hundred thousand names, the index also listed speeches, articles, and other writings.

It was in the 1960s that computers were first employed for surveillance purposes as the FBI began storing information about the arrests of student protesters and other activists. State and federal police forces also moved to computerize criminal records. Today the FBI's Computerized Criminal History system (CCH) stores criminal records as well as the fingerprints of some 70 million individuals, ranging from federal employees to nuclear plant workers. Given the Bureau's history, civil libertarians fear that the CCH might also contain additional detailed information on people whose only "crime" has been participation in a demonstration or travel to a communist country.[28]

In recent years, with the intention of combating fraud against the government, federal, state, and private computer records increasingly have become linked to one another. Congress passed a law in 1984 requiring states to participate in this computer-matching effort. Although the expressed targets of this disturbingly vast system are welfare and Medicaid "cheats," it is clear that the same networks can be used to track citizens who fall into other categories as well.[29] According to Kenneth Laudon, author of *The Dossier Society*, "continued development of state and federal systems presages an automated 'black listing' capability thousands of times more powerful yet considerably more silent than the blacklists of the McCarthy era."[30]

Individual Rights Versus Police Power

Traditionally, Americans have strongly believed in their right to privacy and their right to speak out against government policies. Today, however, the existence of terrorism and instability throughout the world has given the government a pretext for arguing the necessity of unprecedented security measures and incursions against individual rights.

It would be highly unrealistic to deny that every country requires surveillance and intelligence operations. But it is vital to distinguish government programs aimed at criminals and truly dangerous groups (such as the Ku Klux Klan) from the unjustifiable surveillance of law-abiding citizens, including political dissidents.

What the advocates of conformity and carefully regulated dissident opinion forget is that a free society cannot be a heavily controlled society. In their zeal to suppress real and imagined enemies of the status quo, the intelligence agencies and their private allies tend to leave democracy behind and move in the direction of the totalitarian societies they abhor.

Notes

1. Philip S. Foner, *History of the Labor Movement in the United States, Vol. 1. From Colonial Times to the Founding of the American Federation of Labor* (New York: International Publishers, 1962), pp. 460–463.

2. William Seagle, "The American National Police," *Harper's Monthly*, November 1934.

3. Herbert Mitgang, "Annals of Government: Policing America's Writers," *The New Yorker*, 5 October 1987; Natalie Robins, "The Defiling of Writers," *The Nation*, 10 October 1987.

4. Penn Kimball, *The File* (New York: Harcourt Brace Jovanovich, 1983).

5. Frank Donner, *The Age of Surveillance: The Aims and Methods of America's Political Intelligence System* (New York: Random House, 1981), pp. 191–194; "Let Him Wear A Wolf's Head: What the FBI Did to William Albertson," *Civil Liberties Review*, April–May 1976.

6. For more on this, see Donner, p. 288.

7. Ken Lawrence, "The Mississippi Police State—A Report," *ACLU Memo* 5 (March–April 1977).

8. Detailed descriptions of efforts by the FBI and other agencies to harass underground publications are contained in Geoffrey Rips et al., *The Campaign Against the Underground Press*. PEN American Center Report (San Francisco: City Lights, 1981). See also Chip Berlet, "COINTELPRO: The FBI's Zany and Disruptive War on the Alternative Press," *Alternative Media*, Fall 1978.

9. David Armstrong, *A Trumpet to Arms: Alternative Media in America* (Los Angeles: Tarcher, 1981). This news service continues to serve campus publications and today is thought to be free of government involvement.

10. For a good discussion of the work of informants, see Gary T. Marx, "Thoughts on a Neglected Category of Social Movement Participant: The Agent Provocateur and the Informant," *American Journal of Sociology* 80, no. 2 (1974).

11. Articles about the FISA court have regularly complained that it rubber-stamps agency requests. See, for example, "A Court That Never Says No," *The Progressive*, November 1984.

12. "Actor Reagan Was FBI Informant in Red Scare," *Houston Chronicle*, 26 August 1985.

13. Unless otherwise indicated, the following examples are taken from the chronologies of the Center for Constitutional Rights Movement Support Network.

14. Testimony of the Center for Constitutional Rights before the House Committee on the Judiciary, Subcommittee on Civil and Constitutional Rights, 20 February 1987, p. 13.

15. Movement Support Network, "Harassment Update, Twelfth Edition," December 1987.

16. Wayne King, "An FBI Inquiry Fed by Informer Emerges in Analysis of Documents," *The New York Times*, 13 February 1988.

17. See, for example, "Study of 50 Break-Ins Shows No Clear Plot on Policy Critics," *The New York Times*, 19 February 1987.

18. Anthony Schmitz, "The Spy Who Said No," *Mother Jones*, April 1988.

19. "Sources Say North Had Secret Plan for Martial Law," *Philadelphia Inquirer*, 5 July 1987; see also "Return of the Night of the Animals," *The Village Voice*, 26 February 1985.

20. "Alien Terrorists and Undesirables: A Contingency Plan,"

Investigations Division, Immigration and Naturalization Service, U.S. Department of Justice, May 1986.

21. See "Activists Invite a Student, Get a Policeman," *Philadelphia Inquirer*, 5 July 1987.

22. Richard Esposito, "Black Radio, Blue File," *New York Newsday*, 26 October 1987; "Police Admit Surveillance Violated Pact," *The New York Times*, 19 December 1987.

23. See Elton Manzione, "The Private Spy Agency," *National Reporter*, Summer 1985.

24. "Detective in Spying Case Linked to Birch Lead," *Los Angeles Times*, 24 May 1983; "New ACLU Suit Aims at Rightwing Group," *Los Angeles Times*, 19 April 1984. Police departments in other locations are also believed to have transferred files that should have been destroyed to private groups for safekeeping.

25. Joel Bleifuss, "The Right Has Its Eyes on You," *In These Times*, 23 December 1987.

26. "FW Man Says North Backed His Spying on Foes of Contras," *Dallas Morning News*, 5 March 1987.

27. CIA v. Sims, (April 1985). Also disturbing is that the Court in *Sims* made an approving reference to an appellate court's observation that pieces of information, having no innate intelligence value in themselves, may be important in conjunction with other bits of information and thereby justify nondisclosure.

28. Kenneth C. Laudon, in *The Dossier Society* (New York: Columbia University Press, 1986), analyzes the political and value choices associated with the CCH and other national computer systems.

29. Philip Mattera, "Caught in the Crossfile," *The Progressive*, March 1985.

30. Laudon, *The Dossier Society*, pp. 324–325.

Selected Readings

Armstrong, David. *A Trumpet to Arms: Alternative Media in America*. Los Angeles: Tarcher, 1981.

Bamford, James. *The Puzzle Palace: Inside the National Security Agency*. New York: Penguin, 1982.

Blackstock, Nelson. *COINTELPRO: The FBI's Secret War on Political Freedom*. New York: Vintage, 1975.

Donner, Frank. *The Age of Surveillance: The Aims and Methods of America's Political Intelligence System*. New York: Random House, 1981.

Goldstein, Robert J. *Political Repression in Modern America*. Cambridge, MA: Schenkman, 1981.

Halperin, M., and J. Gutman. *The Lawless State: The Crimes of the U.S. Intelligence Agencies*. New York: Penguin, 1976.

Laudon, Kenneth C. *The Dossier Society*. New York: Columbia University Press, 1986.

Richelson, Jeffrey T. *The U.S. Intelligence Community*. Cambridge, MA: Ballinger, 1985.

Rips, Geoffrey, A. Neier, T. Gitlin, and A. Mackenzie. *The Campaign Against the Underground Press*. PEN American Center Report. San Francisco: City Lights, 1981.

Theoharis, Athan. *Spying on Americans: Political Surveillance from Hoover to the Huston Plan*. Philadelphia: Temple University Press, 1978.

Unger, Sanford J. *FBI: An Uncensored Look Behind the Walls*. Boston: Little, Brown, 1975.

Wise, David. *The American Police State*. New York: Random House, 1976.

7

THE TRUTH STOPS HERE

Government Secrecy and Direct Censorship

A popular Government, without popular information, or the means of acquiring it, is but the Prologue to a Farce or a Tragedy; or, perhaps both.
—James Madison

Most people would agree that absolute openness in government is not possible; certain kinds of information inevitably must be withheld. Sometimes the reason is security: In wartime the divulging of military strategy can be disastrous. Another justification is diplomacy: Prematurely revealing negotiating positions can undermine the process of conducting international relations. Practicality and efficiency are other rationales. Early in this nation's history, delegates to the Constitutional Convention decided to close the proceedings in order to prevent outside publicity from impeding the task at hand.

But secrecy can become an addiction for those in power, especially those who work under the pressures of public office. It must therefore be assured that while our leaders and those who execute their policies may often be tempted to operate behind closed doors, the desire to do so is restrained. In theory this restraint is practiced as a matter of course in the United States, where openness has traditionally been cited as one of the great virtues of the American system of government.

This tradition has become more and more remote over the past few decades, however, as successive administrations have promoted secrecy under the banners of executive privilege, national security, and counterterrorism. The momentum of the move toward closed government increased dramatically during the Reagan years.

The National Security State

Though instances of excessive or arbitrary government secrecy in the United States can be found before the 1930s, it was during the administration of Franklin Roosevelt that concealment became a standard feature of federal government operations. Today's tight-lipped executive branch originated with the program to build the first atomic bomb.

The ultrasecret research on the bomb, begun without notification to members of Congress, included the clandestine construction of entire cities that were kept off the map. A powerful military apparatus had come into being, and it soon employed tens of thousands of people and was governed by its own rules and regulations. The scientists who worked on the Manhattan Project were ordered not to divulge the nature of their work. Undercover agents were assigned to all installations, and workers were subject to large fines or jail sentences if they violated security regulations.

Manhattan Project facilities included alarm systems, office vaults to safeguard documents, and "secure" telephones. The rule was that people should not be trusted with more information than they "needed to know" in order to carry out designated tasks. Neither Congress nor the American public was told what was being done, and painstaking efforts were made to ensure that any news of the existence of this research was kept away from the press.

The end of World War II did not bring an end to the preoccupation with security and secrecy. The Atomic Energy Act of 1946 went far beyond earlier regulations by declaring an entire body of knowledge secret. This law applied to all information that fell within the category of "restricted data," including "all data concerning (1) design, manufacture, or utilization of atomic weapons; (2) the production of special nuclear material; or (3) the use of special nuclear material in the production of energy."

In practice, this definition has come to encompass virtually all atomic energy information that officials choose to restrict on grounds of national security, whether generated by the government or by private citizens. This might include a teaching manual on the problems of living in the atomic age, reports about safety problems at nuclear power plants, or studies regarding the cancer risks associated with nuclear energy. As recently as 1979 the Department of Energy relied on this law to enjoin *The Progressive* magazine from publishing an article about the hydrogen bomb that was based entirely on public information.[1]

The most striking difference between the Atomic Energy Act and other secrecy laws is that the others require deliberate decisions to classify specific documents, while under the Atomic Energy Act information is "born classified."

During the 1950s, the cloak of secrecy over nuclear research continued, even though the government decided to promote the commercial exploitation of nuclear materials—a policy announced in President Eisenhower's famous "Atoms for Peace" speech to the United Nations General Assembly. Control over nuclear policy was placed in the hands of the Atomic Energy Commission and the Joint Committee on Atomic Energy, both of which operated in secret.

Congress then passed a law to facilitate private industry's participation in nuclear power development and made available a variety of subsidies. The involvement of the private sector meant that thousands more men and women would have access to nuclear information, but instead of eliminating secrecy restrictions, the Atomic Energy Commission gave access only to those with security clearances.

Security clearance required background checks of differing levels of intrusiveness, depending on the sensitivity of the information at each job level, and pledges of secrecy that were subject to criminal sanctions. Before long, thousands of people working in science and engineering had been "cleared." Each was sworn not to divulge classified information under any condition unless the person requesting it had a verifiable "need to know."

This secrecy system relied primarily on self-censorship and on the fragmentation of knowledge into discrete units to ensure that only a few people knew the complete dimensions of a particular project. It is estimated that out of the 150,000 people employed to work on the Manhattan Project, only a dozen knew the totality of the program's objectives.[2] Long after nuclear energy had entered the commercial marketplace and could no longer be considered a state secret, these practices persisted. Their main effect was to inhibit informed public debate on the use and hazards of nuclear materials, and to set a broad precedent for the propriety of strict government control of information.

Anticommunism and the Expansion of Executive Power

The other face of secrecy is censorship. The centralization of power that resulted from the move to secrecy was also manifest in attempts to limit the speech of those with divergent ideas—a desire that was most explicit in the tide of anticommunist sentiment that arose after World War II.

In 1940 Congress passed the Smith Alien Registration Act, which made it illegal for anyone to teach or advocate the overthrow of the government by force, or to organize or join any group teaching such a doctrine. With the end of World War II, fear about a "Red Menace" resumed; heightened by the FBI's well-publicized searches for subversion, this fear soon reached epidemic proportions.

In 1949 the Truman administration invoked the Smith Act to convict eleven leading Communist Party officials merely for their membership in the organization; two years later the Supreme Court upheld the convictions and found the act constitutional.[3] No longer was it necessary for an action to have been taken or for a clear and present danger to be shown to the nation's security before the government could punish those who held dissenting views.

Attempts to criminalize certain beliefs were also furthered by the passage of the McCarran Internal Security Act in 1950. This legislation required all members of the Communist Party to register with the attorney general, forbade aliens who had been party members to enter the country, barred them from working in defense plants and from getting passports, and authorized the president to hold them in detention camps in the event of war. President Truman, charging that this measure punished opinion rather than action, vetoed it, but he was overridden.

Then followed the witch-hunt in Congress brewed by Senator Joseph McCarthy of Wisconsin.[4] The congressional hearings gave those subpoenaed to appear the choice of agreeing to testify, in which case they could not limit their testimony to their own beliefs and associations, or refusing to testify by invoking the Fifth Amendment, thereby depriving themselves of the option of pleading innocent. Those called for investigation included federal employees, people who worked in films and television, and members of the academic world, many of whom were subsequently fired and blacklisted in their professions as dangerous subversives. The climate of suspicion grew, and local inquisitions sprang up around the country. Librarians were pressured and intimidated for placing the books of certain authors on the shelves; professors were harassed for holding unconventional views.[5]

Covert Operations and Secret Wars

The Cold War offensive proceeded abroad as well as at home, and the expansion of covert operations overseas also helped to engender a culture of secrecy. American foreign policy developed what Blanche Wiesen Cook, author of *The Declassified Eisenhower*, calls a top side and an underside: The top side avowed a commitment to peace, while the underside waged an ongoing political war against those who did not align themselves with American ideology.[6]

In 1954, the National Security Council made this bifurcated strategy explicit in a directive that stated that "in the interests of world peace and U.S. national security, the overt foreign activities of the U.S. Government should be supplemented by covert operations." Responsibility for covert activities was placed largely in the hands of the CIA, which took its mandate to include secretly interfering with elections and other domestic political activities in foreign countries. Cook notes that the NSC directive "ended all pretensions about territorial integrity, national sovereignty and international law. Covert operatives were everywhere, and they were active. From bribery to assassination, no activity was unacceptable short of nuclear war."

In the 1960s the covert and overt aspects of United States foreign policy came together in Vietnam. For many years the full extent of U.S. involvement in Southeast Asia was kept secret from the American people, and even once the country was clearly at war—though Congress never issued a formal declaration—military leaders tightly controlled information about its course. Perhaps the greatest deception was President Nixon's secret extension of the war into Cambodia.

Among the central issues of the Watergate scandal that brought the Nixon administration to an end were secrecy, censorship (in the form of "dirty tricks"), and the consolidation of power in the executive branch. President Nixon's invocation of executive privilege as a reason for withholding information from Congress, including the claim that the president could order anyone in his administration not to testify on any subject, showed how far the nation had drifted toward autocracy.

The Reagan Years

From its beginnings, the Reagan administration made little attempt to disguise its preference for operating outside congressional and public scrutiny; it quickly adopted an array of secrecy regulations that reached far beyond those of previous administrations. Moreover, the significant expansion of the Pentagon's role during the Reagan presidency extended military secrecy rules far into the civilian sector, including universities, research laboratories, and diverse businesses that perform work for the government.[7]

That concealing information has become a habit of the federal government was most visible in the area of classification. Some experts on national security regulation have described the classification of documents as nothing more than a program of news management, used to distract attention from real secrets. The first executive order on classification was adopted by Franklin Roosevelt in 1940; its purpose was to protect information pertaining to military installations. Since then, with some intervening attempts at limiting the volume and duration of classified material, the scope of classification has been broadened considerably.

Under President Nixon, the number of people who had the power to classify documents was substantially reduced. Timetables ranging from six to thirty years were established for the automatic declassification of materials, and for once, private citizens were given the right to request review of classification that had been continued past the deadline.[8]

The Carter administration added further safeguards against excessive secrecy. For the first time, it was specified that only particular categories of material could be classified, and that decisions to withhold information be limited to those materials which, if released, could reasonably be expected to cause "identifiable damage" to the national security. Moreover, the Carter policy required the use of a balancing test in each instance to determine if the public interest in disclosure outweighed the government's secrecy interest.

The Reagan administration veered sharply in the opposite

direction. Most of the reforms of the Nixon and Carter years were undone in a new executive order issued in 1982. It did away with the balancing test and instead instructed agency personnel that when in doubt they should classify. The order did not recognize a need to identify damage to the national security, and it eliminated a prohibition against reclassifying documents that had previously been declassified and released under the Freedom of Information Act. Further, it provided that information could now remain classified indefinitely and without review.

The Reagan policy also significantly expanded the number of officials empowered to make classification determinations. Under this system, a wide variety of government bureaucrats, acting as a sort of "classification priesthood," are allowed to make what are considered routine decisions but are in fact helping to determine the contours of American democracy.[9]

Floyd Abrams, a leading constitutional lawyer, commented early in the Reagan years that this administration "acts as if information were in the nature of a potentially disabling disease which must be feared, controlled and ultimately quarantined." This attitude has manifested itself not only in the expansion of the scope of classified material, but also in attempts to extend secrecy restrictions to categories of *unclassified* material.

The origin of this bizarre concept was in the "born classified" approach of the Atomic Energy Act. A 1982 article in *The Bulletin of the Atomic Scientists* argued that this policy, adopted in emergency wartime conditions, should be withdrawn, since "the precedent lies around like a loaded gun awaiting use in other spheres."[10] Not long after this article was published, the Department of Energy proved how well grounded this concern was by creating a category of "unclassified controlled nuclear information" (UCNI), which Congress duly codified in an amendment to the Atomic Energy Act.

The definition of UCNI included information concerning defense programs that "could reasonably be expected to have a significant adverse effect on the health and safety of the public," which, not coincidentally, could also be of great interest to the public as a consequence.

Then, in September 1984, President Reagan issued a directive on improving the protection of federal telecommunications and automated information systems. These systems were highly susceptible to unauthorized access by terrorist groups and foreign nations, it asserted, and called for tighter security for systems handling "sensitive, but unclassified information" in electronic form, "the loss of which could adversely affect the national security interest."

The directive sparked immediate controversy and was widely regarded as another step in the administration's efforts to extend information restrictions into new areas. It reinforced the conclusions of a (classified) study by the Air Force on national security issues relating to databases available to the public, justifying the extension of controls on the grounds that pieces of certain unclassified data could be put together in ways that would reveal classified information. By stating that the federal government "shall encourage, advise, and, where appropriate, assist the private sector" in identifying systems that handle "sensitive non-government information," the directive seemed to extend government control of information to data stored by private entities.

At a hearing several months later, Ken Allen of the Information Industry Association expressed strong skepticism about the administration's approach. Questioning whether it was possible to define the body of information relevant to the administration's "mosaic" theory, Allen noted that the directive marked the first attempt to establish a broad category of "sensitive but unclassified information." He found the plan to "assist" private industry ominous in light of other government actions, including:

> Intelligence agency visits to private information companies asking questions about their users; the public statements by government officials stating their concerns about foreign access to "NEXIS-type systems"; a government request for private sector customer lists; an Administration proposal to exempt technical data under the Freedom of Information Act; and a secret Air Force report based on interviews with commercial information companies and entitled "Exploitation of Western databases."[11]

As part of its campaign to control unclassified information, the Reagan administration also gave the Pentagon and the National Security Agency authority to set security standards for data contained in all computerized government files. The danger of this was noted by Congressman Jack Brooks, who remarked that "the NSA has a propensity and a tendency to classify everything."[12]

Controversy over the directive reached a peak in October

1986 with the release of a memorandum by then National Security Adviser John Poindexter. The memorandum noted that Poindexter's definition of sensitive but unclassified data encompassed a "wide range of government or government-derived economic, human, financial, industrial, agricultural, technological, and law enforcement information." It was widely regarded as authorization for a new program of extraordinary official concealment.

The policy created a public uproar, forcing the White House to rescind the memorandum and conduct a review of the directive. But the danger remained. The directive was only one piece of a much larger program, and even as the Poindexter memorandum was withdrawn, restrictions on unclassified material continued to come from other offices.

In one example, the Defense Department received permission from Congress in 1984 to withhold from public knowledge data with applications to the military and to outer space. The rationale here was that if technical information in these areas was sensitive enough to require approval before it could be sent abroad, the very existence of the information should remain secret—whether or not it was being considered for export.[13] This new exemption has the potential of greatly reducing the Defense Department's obligation to reveal information about military operations in space. And in fact it was used by then Defense Secretary Caspar Weinberger in 1985 to restrict information given out to the press regarding the planned military payload aboard one of the space shuttle flights.

Declaring War on the Freedom of Information Act

The Reagan administration's assault on openness was particularly harmful to the Freedom of Information Act, the nation's central access law. Before it was adopted in 1966—and strengthened in 1974 during a period of major revelations of government misconduct—citizens' requests for government information were handled arbitrarily. FOIA established a right to obtain all government information that did not fall under the coverage of enumerated exemptions.[14]

FOIA has enabled journalists, historians, and others to uncover a wide range of information. Documents released under it have revealed the FBI harassment of Dr. Martin Luther King, Jr.;

the long history of illegal CIA and FBI monitoring and disruption of domestic political groups; safety problems at nuclear power plants; lax federal enforcement of environmental and civil rights laws; and FBI surveillance of dozens of prominent writers.[15]

The value of FOIA depends to a significant extent on the attitude of the president currently in office. Under the law, documents can be withheld only if they meet the criteria of an administration's classification policy; thus the Reagan administration's penchant for secrecy put large quantities of information out of reach.

The Reagan administration was tireless in its efforts to weaken the FOIA, particularly by adding numerous new categories of exemptions.[16] Congress was induced to endorse this effort. In 1985 the House and Senate, with active encouragement from the White House, passed legislation that excluded from FOIA coverage the operational files of the CIA.[17]

Some of the greatest damage has been inflicted through the bureaucratic procedures that have been practiced in responding to FOIA requests. FOIA requires certain time limits for responses, but many agencies have not taken them seriously; particular agencies and departments have become notorious among applicants and attorneys for long delays as well as for falsely denying the existence of requested information.

Even explicit reminders from Congress of the pro-disclosure thrust of FOIA have been converted into opportunities for denying access. In 1986, for example, new FOIA fee provisions were passed that emphasized that the news media should not be charged for document searches. The intention of lawmakers was to counteract narrow fee-waiver guidelines promulgated by the Justice Department in 1983.[18] Nonetheless, a subsequent Justice Department memorandum claimed that the new provisions were more restrictive than its own guidelines and, with assistance from the Office of Management and Budget, advised agencies to limit fee waivers to people employed by major media organizations and writing about current events.

Testifying before Congress in 1987, Scott Armstrong, a veteran reporter and director of the National Security Archive, summed up the ways in which the Reagan administration was trying to thwart effective use of FOIA. He described the administrative barriers as "presently insurmountable for an individual requester who does not have five years, $20,000 to $100,000 for legal fees, and infinite patience."[19]

Secrecy by Contract

In one of its most stunning—and disturbing—legal victories, the Reagan administration brought an espionage case against a government employee who shared classified material with a news publication, and won. In 1985, Samuel Loring Morison, who worked at the U.S. Naval Intelligence Support Center in Maryland and free-lanced for London-based *Jane's Defense Weekly*, became the first person in the nation's history to be branded as a spy for leaking government information to the press.

The administration also looked for a more comprehensive approach to discourage leaks. In 1983 it introduced the most sweeping censorship controls in the nation's history through the issuance of secrecy contracts that were binding on hundreds of thousands of government workers.

National Security Decision Directive 84 required all federal employees with access to "sensitive compartmented information" to sign nondisclosure agreements that included provisions for the pre-publication review of all writings that the signers might produce for the rest of their lives. Employees were also required to submit to polygraph examinations during the investigation of information leaks. What was most chilling about the directive was that the agreement covered not only classified information but also *classifiable* material—in other words, anything that the government might decide it wanted to keep secret. These agreements are a blatant violation of the free speech rights of a large number of American citizens.[20]

Secrecy contracts requiring pre-publication review were not entirely novel; they had existed for some time in the intelligence community. However, the new directive extended this requirement into the civil service, deliberately muzzling workers who were likely to know about a wide variety of government programs. Similar contracts were soon issued for people outside government whose work depended on federal funds.[21]

The plan was implemented with great speed, but it drew little public comment. In 1986 a study by the General Accounting Office found that some 300,000 people had signed nondisclosure agreements. The estimate was incomplete because the White House, the Office of Management and Budget, and certain other agencies did not submit data. The GAO study also found that the number of polygraph tests administered had risen steadily.

The actions of the Reagan administration were all the more

disturbing for its failure to cite legal authority for such extreme measures. The sole precedent was taken from a Supreme Court decision in 1980 upholding the conviction of former CIA agent Frank Snepp for publishing unclassified information without submitting his manuscript for pre-publication review—as was stipulated in a secrecy contract he had signed.[22]

The tide began to turn against the secrecy contracts in 1987, when the policy was challenged in a lawsuit brought by two federal employee unions, and Congress passed a law prohibiting the administration from spending money to implement or enforce the new nondisclosure contracts during the 1988 fiscal year. Nonetheless, unless these contracts are permanently prohibited by the courts or Congress, they will remain an insidious device for any administration that seeks to silence speech without resorting to more visible forms of censorship.

Deceit out of Control: The Iran-Contra Case

The eleven weeks of hearings in 1987 on the sale of arms to Iran and the diversion of profits to the Nicaraguan contras revealed that an elaborate extragovernmental network had been created. While previous administrations had at times turned to outside assistance to carry out their programs, never before had there been evidence that such an extensive "shadow government" had been used to thwart the will of Congress.

In the most famous Supreme Court decision on the separation of powers, made when President Truman seized the country's steel mills during the Korean War, a president's authority to act apart from Congress was ruled to be least when his actions contradicted policy written into law. In the Iran-Contra initiative, the Reagan administration did precisely this, deliberately creating an organization that tried to operate as if the legislative branch of government did not exist.

The report issued after the Iran-contra hearings cited numerous areas in which the administration had pursued two strategies, one a fiction for public consumption and other the actual covert operation. These included:

• The public policy not to make concessions for the release of hostages, and to exhort other governments to follow suit—while the White House authorized the secret trading of arms for hostages.

• The public policy to ban arms shipments to Iran—while sophisticated missiles were secretly being sold to that country.

• The public policy to conduct covert operations solely through the CIA or intelligence programs specifically authorized by the president—while the White House made extensive use of private, nonaccountable agents for covert operations, under the leadership of staff at the National Security Council, who deliberately kept the president uninformed to limit his accountability.

• The public policy contained in agreements signed by then CIA Director William Casey to consult with the appropriate congressional committees about covert operations—while covert programs were secretly expanded and Casey repeatedly lied to committee members.

• The public policy to obey the "letter and spirit" of the Boland Amendment's ban on military aid to the contras—while an elaborate program was created to provide continuing military aid and strategy in secret.[23]

As the Iran-contra events unfolded, hyperbole and partial truths were employed as public relations tools before, during, and after news of the arms sales and the diversion of profits had surfaced. Officials all the way up to the president suffered chronic losses of memory; one high-ranking official admitted lying to members of Congress. Evidence was destroyed; as Oliver North and others carted large piles of documents to the shredder, passive Justice Department employees stood by.

Admiral John Poindexter testified that he destroyed the only existing copy of a 1985 Presidential Finding on the arms-for-hostages operation to spare the president political embarrassment. Such findings, according to Congress's final report on the matter, were used to "enhance control over covert action operations," and to "justify an evasion of one of the Constitution's more fundamental safeguards, the dependence of the executive branch upon Congress for specific appropriations."[24]

While Reagan was still in office, the special prosecutor announced criminal charges against some of the initiative's leaders, but the president asserted that no law had been violated, arousing public speculation that this extraordinary "shadow government" might go unrepudiated. Nonetheless, North was tried and convicted on three of twelve counts. Still, it is not clear that the federal government has learned its lesson about the consequences of executive branch secrecy and unilateral action.

The danger of a closed government is apparent to all of us who are aware of its inevitable results, including some advocates of a stronger military. Edward Teller has written:

> Rapid progress cannot be reconciled with central control and secrecy. The limitations we impose on ourselves by restricting information are far greater than any advantage others could gain by copying our ideas.... Adopting a policy of openness ... would strengthen our relationships with our allies as well as illustrate the advantages of freedom to our Soviet colleagues.[25]

Teller's wisdom is a rarity in both of our major political parties, where the impulse toward secrecy and censorship continues to thrive. The task now is to abandon the preoccupation with the national security state and recognize that openness is indeed the foundation of strength.

Notes

1. Publication of the article "The H Bomb Secret: How We Got It, Why We're Telling It," was held up for six months after a federal district court agreed with the government that it contained restricted data. It finally appeared in the November 1979 issue of *The Progressive.*
2. See "The Pentagon and the Scientists," in John Tirman, ed., *The Militarization of High Technology* (Cambridge, MA: Ballinger, 1985), p. 153.
3. Dennis v. United States, 341 U.S. 494 (1951).
4. Bertram Gross, author of *Friendly Fascism: The New Face of Power in America* (Boston: South End, 1980), p. 88, reminds us that the purges of the McCarthy era were preceded by other House

committees. The first one, established in the 1930s, investigated Nazi activities in the U.S. and other forms of subversive propaganda. When its authority expired, it was replaced by another committee that "launched a vigorous attack on alleged radicals in government, on the more liberal members of President Roosevelt's cabinet, and on the more liberal and radical trade unions then represented by the newly organized CIO." After the war ended, this so-called special House Un-American Activities Committee was made a standing body, as opposed to one of limited duration.

5. Jack Nelson, *Censors in the Schools* (Westport, CT: Greenwood, 1977).

6. Blanche Wiesen Cook, *The Declassified Eisenhower* (New York: Penguin, 1981), p. 183.

7. According to some of the leading experts on arms control, the Pentagon is now the principal economic influence in the United States. For more on this, see "The Defense-Economy Debate," in Tirman.

8. Executive Order 11652, 1972.

9. The Reagan classification order lists the following government information as eligible for classification: "(1) military plans, weapons or operations; (2) the vulnerabilities or capabilities of systems, installations, projects or plans relating to the national security; (3) foreign government information; (4) intelligence activities (including special activities, or intelligence sources or methods); (5) foreign relations or foreign activities of the United States; (6) scientific, technological or economic matters relating to the national security; (7) United States government programs for safeguarding nuclear materials or facilities; (8) cryptology; (9) a confidential source; or (10) other categories of information that are related to the national security and that require protection against unauthorized disclosure as determined by the President or by agency heads or other officials who have been delegated original classification authority by the President" (Executive Order No. 12356, 1982).

10. Mary M. Cheh, "Atoms for Peace. Secrecy: Why Is It Still With Us?" *The Bulletin of the Atomic Scientists*, December 1982, p. 66.

11. Testimony of Kenneth B. Allen, Senior Vice-President, Government Relations, Information Industry Association, before the National Commission on Libraries and Information Science, 28 May 1987.

12. In late 1987, however, Congress passed legislation shifting control back to civilian hands, namely the National Bureau of Standards.

13. The restrictions on information contained in export regulations are discussed in chapter 10.

14. These exemptions include: (1) national security information; (2) agency rules and practices; (3) information Congress has declared confidential through other statutes; (4) confidential business information; (5) interagency or intra–agency memoranda;

(6) personnel or medical files; (7) law enforcement investigations; 8) banking reports; and (9) information about oil and gas wells.

15. Herbert Mitgang, "Annals of Government: Policing America's Writers," *The New Yorker*, 5 October 1987; Natalie Robins, "The Defiling of Writers," *The Nation*, 10 October 1987.

16. Reagan's classification order added the capabilities and vulnerabilities of military systems, projects, or plans; confidential sources; and cryptology to the earlier list that included military plans, weapons, or operations; intelligence activities, sources, and methods; information about foreign governments; U.S. foreign relations; scientific, technological, or economic matters relating to national security; and programs for safeguarding nuclear materials or facilities.

17. The administrations also successfully lobbied for a law, passed in 1982, makes it a crime to reveal the names of U.S. intelligence agents, even if the information is public and unclassified.

18. Freedom of Information Reform Act of 1986, Pub. L. No. 99-570. The law required that only persons seeking documents for commercial use pay full search and copying costs, and also waived search fees for educational and scientific institutions.

19. Testimony of Scott Armstrong, Executive Director of the National Security Archive, before the Government Information, Justice and Agriculture Subcommittee of the House Committee on Government Operations, 2 December 1987.

20. Angus Mackenzie, "The Big Chill," *The Quill*, March 1984; and "Fit To Be Tied," *The Quill*, July/August 1985. Donna Demac, "Sworn to Silence," *The Progressive*, May 1987.

21. Classified Information Nondisclosure Agreement Standard Form 189A, issued in November 1986.

22. Frank W. Snepp III v. United States, 444 U.S. 507 (1980).

23. *Report of the Congressional Committees Investigating the Iran-contra Affair.* U.S. Senate Committee on Secret Military Assistance to Iran and the Nicaraguan Opposition and the U.S. House Select Committee to Investigate Covert Arms Transactions with Iran, November 1987.

24. Ibid., p. 380.

25. Edward Teller, "Secrecy: The Road to Nowhere," *Technology Review*, October 1981.

Selected Readings

American Library Association. *Less Access to Less Information By and About the U.S. Government* (a chronology). Washington, DC: ALA, 1982–1988.

Demac, Donna. *Keeping America Uninformed: Government Secrecy in the 1980s.* New York: Pilgrim, 1984.

Department of Defense Commission to Review DOD Security Policies and Practices (Report of). *Keeping the Nation's Secrets.* Washington, DC: Department of Defense, 19 November 1985.

Dorsen, Norman, and S. Gillers, eds. *None of Your Business: Government Secrecy in America.* New York: Penguin, 1975.

Ford, Daniel. *The Cult of the Atom: The Secret Papers of the Atomic Energy Commission.* New York: Simon and Schuster, 1984.

Galnoor, Itzhak, ed. *Government Secrecy in Democracies.* New York: Harper & Row, 1977.

Gross, Bertram. *Friendly Fascism: The New Face of Power in America.* Boston: South End, 1980.

Hilgartner, Stephen, R. C. Bell, and R. O'Connor. *Nukespeak: The Selling of Nuclear Technology in America.* San Francisco: Sierra Club, 1982.

Pell, Eve. *The Big Chill.* Boston: Beacon, 1984.

Tirman, John, ed. The *Militarization of High Technology.* Cambridge, MA: Ballinger, 1985.

8

CENSORS IN THE SHADOWS

Bureaucratic Restrictions
on Information

*This is the most closed government since the founding of the
American republic, and no one knows it. We're talking
about information, the most important government service.*
—Sheldon Samuels, former AFL-CIO Director of Safety and
Health.

The perpetrators of government censorship and secrecy are not
limited to FBI agents and White House aides with little respect
for the Constitution. Over the past dozen years, and especially
during the Reagan administration, the assault on freedom of
expression and openness in government has also been carried out
by scores of officials working within the sprawling federal
bureaucracy. Acting in the name of budget cutting, deregulation,
and paperwork reduction, this army of bureaucrats has succeeded not in promoting efficiency, but rather in denying Americans access to a vast array of information.

The elements of this administrative censorship—promoted
for the most part by executive branch fiat rather than legislation—include the following:

• making it more difficult for public groups to gain access
to the documents of regulatory agencies;
• scaling back data-collection programs in areas such as
industry compliance with environmental laws;
• privatizing libraries of federal agencies, thus making
material less accessible to the public;
• eliminating thousands of federal publications, some of
which were the only low-cost sources of information on
subjects like medical care and consumer protection.

Although such decisions involve actions by officials in dozens of executive branch agencies, the main force behind administrative censorship and secrecy is the Office of Management and Budget. Most Americans who know of the OMB at all think of it only as the agency that draws up the budget proposal presented by the president to Congress each year. But in recent years the OMB has become an important influence in determining domestic policy. Under the Reagan administration this agency became the Trojan horse for the conservative effort to dismantle large sections of the federal apparatus and to render the remaining programs less susceptible to public participation. Gary Bass, director of the public interest group OMB Watch, has said that the OMB "has become the meat ax. It can bypass Congress and the courts and go straight into the agencies to do its work. It's Reagan's best tool."[1]

One's eyes tend to glaze over at the mention of administrative matters. But behind seemingly bland discussions of rule-making procedures, paperwork "burden hours," and cost/benefit ratios are fundamental issues regarding the nature of government. The idea of paperwork reduction sounds harmless, even laudable, yet its implementation has included such "reforms" as the easing of reporting requirements for corporations manufacturing hazardous products. What is for industry a welcome reduction of red tape is for the public a potential obstacle to effective organizing on the issue of toxic waste.

Like the bureaucratic language Newspeak in George Orwell's *1984*, the vocabulary of administrative censorship obscures government policies and creates a false unity around the drive to narrow the scope of government. The assertion of a universal desire to "get Washington off our backs" cloaks a process in which the federal government is simultaneously abandoning essential functions and undermining public access and participation.

The Town Crier Writ Large

Information was considered important to American society long before it was central to government operations. The Founding Fathers regarded an electorate that was well informed about the activities of government as an essential part of the democratic vision and an important element of government accountability.

The Constitution contains several provisions that focus on the sharing of information. The president is to make an annual address on the state of the nation; information should flow from the executive to Congress in the oversight process; and Congress is required to "keep a journal of its proceedings and from time to time publish the same, excepting such parts as may in their judgment require secrecy." The First Amendment establishes the public's right to exchange information and ideas without government interference.

Early in the country's history, Congress passed laws making its documents available to universities, historical societies, and the legislatures of the states. The Depository Library System, created in the nineteeth century, established a program in which federal documents are supplied without cost to a group of libraries (now numbering some 1,400), so long as the institutions make them freely accessible to the public.

About a century ago, the federal government became a major data collector as well as an important source of information about its own activities. In addition to the constitutionally mandated census of the population, the federal government took on a slew of other information-gathering responsibilities. It established the Bureau of Labor Statistics, for instance, in 1884.

As the era of laissez-faire gave way to government regulation of business, federal agencies began requiring companies to disclose more of the data needed to monitor their activities. This information collection took on greater urgency with news of scandalous industry practices. *The Jungle,* Upton Sinclair's 1906 exposé of conditions in the meat-packing industry, helped move Congress to initiate food and drug regulation, which included provisions for the government to gather information and share it with the public.

Throughout the twentieth century the federal government's information activities have expanded in tandem with its regulatory functions. Though some federal agencies developed sweetheart relations with the industries they regulated, requirements that companies submit information on a regular basis ensured at least a minimum level of industry accountability. In addition, laws passed by Congress made the entire process open to public scrutiny.

Public Rights in Agency Proceedings

The basic framework for agency rule-making was established in the 1946 Administrative Procedure Act.[2] The act contains rules applicable to most agency actions and is intended to ensure that proceedings will be open and conducted according to established procedures. These include the requirement that an agency contemplating rule changes issue a Notice of Proposed Rulemaking alerting the public of the matter to be considered; establish times in the proceeding for public comment; and publish the text of the final rule, along with an explanation of its purpose. Agency notices and decisions are published in the *Federal Register*, the most comprehensive record of ongoing agency activities.

These procedures became of vital importance in the 1960s, when a new generation of political activists turned their attention to the federal government to promote their goals in areas like civil rights and environmental protection. Many of the period's most controversial issues were addressed through regulatory channels. Public interest groups found that they could gain a comprehensive understanding of industry practices through information made available in the course of agency proceedings and that, on the basis of such information, they could intervene more effectively in the process to bring about reforms. Media activists, for example, used data collected by the FCC to determine how broadcasters were responding to contemporary pressures to increase the number of minority employees in the industry.

The Freedom of Information Act was also a major tool in the public's ability to scrutinize the administrative activities of the federal government. The act imposed an affirmative obligation on agencies to make available information about their operations, including procedures for participation in agency proceedings and the texts of all final opinions.[3]

Once regulatory and administrative decisions became objects of public scrutiny, with subsequent media attention, the White House moved to expand its control. The Nixon administration took the first decisive step in this direction by transforming the Bureau of the Budget into the Office of Management and Budget and centralizing a great deal of executive branch decision-making under the OMB.

Within a few years, however, a reorientation took place in the regulatory and administrative landscape. By the mid-1970s the business community had launched an all-out counterattack on the federal bureaucracy. Companies like Mobil Oil spent huge sums assailing government regulation, which was now depicted as an impediment to economic growth. Special venom was directed at the newer areas of social regulation—workplace health, consumer products safety, and the like—that forced industry to assume broader responsibility for the welfare of employees and the public.

The ideological success of the business effort was seen most clearly in the passage of the Paperwork Reduction Act of 1980. The problem of bureaucratic red tape is undeniable, but the way in which this law has been used is a classic example of throwing out the baby with the bathwater. Many of the supposedly superfluous reporting requirements eliminated under the law were actually essential data-gathering efforts concerning industry practices as well as trends in areas like health and housing.

The law also put even more power in the hands of the OMB. It created a new Office of Information and Regulatory Affairs within the agency and gave it primary responsibility not only for paperwork reduction but also for data collection, statistical analysis, privacy protection, and the automation of agency programs. OIRA soon emerged as the chief dragon among the regulatory and administrative marauders who were put in place following the election of Ronald Reagan.

The Reaganites in the Chicken Coop

The Reagan administration's affirmative disregard for the aims of open government and an informed public led to the design of a complex program to place enormous amounts of information off limits and to restrict what remained in government files. The regulatory and administrative campaign was joined with a thorough revamping of fiscal policies. The overall thrust has been described by former OMB director David Stockman:

> To put across goals of a military build-up, tax cuts and a balanced budget called for trench-style political warfare. . . . Forty years' worth of promises, subventions, entitlements, and safety nets issued by the federal government would have to be scrapped or drastically modified.[4]

112

Just as the federal government was no longer to be a major source of economic aid and protection, so it was to abandon its role as a provider of information. State governments, hospitals, universities, and even corporations that relied on the federal government for statistics could no longer depend on Washington. At most executive branch agencies, representatives of business had far more success than the general public with direct inquiries, though they too encountered indifference regarding the unavailability of information the government had previously supplied.

Coordinating this shift in policy was OIRA, which for the first five years of the Reagan administration was headed by Douglas Ginsburg (later the failed Supreme Court nominee). Executive orders adopted in 1982 and 1985 put OIRA at the forefront of two pillars of the Reagan revolution: deregulation and the privatization of government programs.[5]

The Circumlocution Office

Desk officers at OIRA, assigned to review agency programs, vetoed plans for new publications, delayed proceedings with statutory time limits, and often conferred confidentially with industry groups. Keeping a low profile, OIRA quietly and systematically worked to transform the federal government into an entity that resembled a closed and inaccessible fortress. It became an all-too-real version of the Circumlocution Office Dickens portrayed in *Little Dorrit*.

One example of the power the OMB exercised was seen in 1986, when OIRA vetoed plans by the Environmental Protection Agency to conduct a survey of certain chemicals in drinking water. Previous studies had suggested that there was a link between the ingestion of chlorine, for instance, and health hazards. In rejecting this study, OIRA proclaimed: "What is the practical utility of the information? What will EPA do with either a positive confirmation or negative confirmation of a relationship in humans?"[6]

The cost/benefit standard used by OIRA to evaluate programs required agencies to put a dollar value on the potential benefit to human life. The near impossibility of doing so made it virtually inevitable that these benefits would be outweighed by the more easily calculated cost of new or expanded regulations.

113

Another indication of the power exercised by the OMB is the time agencies must now spend defending their own course of action. Ironically, the agency that is supposed to be promoting paperwork reduction has greatly expanded the number of forms that other executive branch offices must fill out.

A partial list of reports that must be submitted to the OMB includes an annual draft regulatory program, semi-annual agendas of planned regulations and existing rules, and periodic assessments of the general economic costs and benefits of all regulatory proposals, along with justification for their continuation. For every rule of any significance, agencies must file a Regulatory Impact Analysis that compares the costs and benefits of its proposal with those of alternative approaches. In contrast to the early-notification provisions of various federal laws, agencies are now prohibited from publishing their proposed and final rules until the completion of OMB review.[7]

Agencies must also participate in the development of the OMB's two budgets: the annual federal budget and its own Information Collection Budget.[8] Through the latter the OMB reviews the paperwork "burden hours" created by regulatory activities and then establishes limits for each agency. Thus the information budget—developed with the stated aim of reducing government paperwork—has actually been used by OIRA to advance deregulation and to phase out the federal government's role as a data provider. Rather than serve as a leading source of information on vital public issues, the Reagan government was the reluctant provider of last resort.

As a result of the OMB's new role, the most important elements of agency deliberations have come to be conducted outside public and congressional scrutiny. On numerous occasions, the OMB has delayed final action well beyond a statutory deadline, forcing public interest groups to file lawsuits to speed up the proceedings.

In a case with an extra twist, the Environmental Defense Fund sued the EPA for its failure to meet a congressionally imposed deadline for dealing with toxic leaks from underground storage tanks. It also challenged the OMB, claiming that it had delayed action by the EPA and "routinely contravened the commands of Congress." Seeking to limit publicity, the OMB claimed that certain documents concerning its deliberations with the EPA were confidential, and obtained a court order that restricted circulation of the documents. When the environmental group made limited reference to these documents in its brief, the government demanded that it be recalled and refiled it under seal. The court denied this motion, calling it "extraordinary and unwarranted," and noted that there was no way the case could be conducted openly if the request were granted.[9] Eventually the court ruled against the OMB.

Other federal agencies have made it clear that public participation is not welcome, by no longer publishing many of their notices, reports, and bulletins—a policy in direct violation of the Freedom of Information Act.[10] In other instances agencies have delayed the publication of documents or failed to keep them at the places where the public is supposed to be able to gain access to them.[11]

In keeping with the patchwork nature of bureaucratic control, agencies have used numerous discrete actions to limit access to information. The Federal Communications Commission, for example, dramatically reduced the amount of information available on broadcaster performance by:

- reducing the length of broadcast renewal applications from more than ten pages to the size of a postcard;
- ending the requirement for stations to submit sample program logs and data on the quantity of their commercials, their public service announcements, and their public affairs programming;
- dropping the requirement that stations make documents available for public inspection.

Moreover, in 1986 the FCC announced that instead of publishing the full texts of its proceeding notices in the *Federal Register*, it would henceforth publish only summaries.

The OMB Versus Congress

The OMB's running battles with Congress during the Reagan administration included many attempts to block access to information by congressional oversight committees. Refusals to turn over information regarding the EPA's toxic waste program resulted in 1983 in the first contempt-of-Congress citation of a federal official. Although the EPA was bound by congressional laws that included specific deadlines for remedial actions, the

OMB repeatedly thwarted statutory objectives by delaying EPA proceedings—a technique it used to hold back the programs at other agencies as well.

The OMB entered the political scene in other ways. It has acted to prevent information from reaching Congress by limiting the advocacy that groups receiving federal funds could engage in. Strong opposition from many members of Congress (and even industry representatives) caused the OMB to modify the proposal, but it did not stop the issuance of new rules that generated much confusion among organizations and potential funders as to the acceptable range of actions that came under the heading of "advocacy."[12]

Congress shares some of the blame for the OMB actions that have undermined the ability of the public to know what the government is doing. Not only have the legislators refused to challenge the OMB's encroachments seriously, but they reauthorized the Paperwork Reduction Act in 1986 without placing significant limits on the Office of Information and Regulatory Affairs. Less than two years later, OIRA showed its lack of gratitude by "interpreting" recent congressional amendments to the Freedom of Information Act intended to encourage fee waivers in a way that in fact limits those who are eligible for the waivers.

Congress itself has also been guilty of actions that have worked against keeping the public informed. In the name of cutting the budget, public access to the House and Senate document rooms was limited, and restrictions were placed on the number of copies of bills, committee reports, and hearing records made available for public distribution.

The legislative branch was also responsible for approving budget cuts in 1986 that led to severe reductions in the hours of the public reading room of the Library of Congress, as well as a thirteen-percent cut in the Library's acquisitions budget and the loss of three hundred staff positions. After persistent protests, including sit-ins by library patrons, the reading-room schedule was restored.

Not Fit to Print: Eliminating Publications and Statistics

Soon after taking office in 1981, President Reagan issued a moratorium on new government publications. Over the next six years some twenty-five percent of federal publications went out of print. Among these were *Health Care Financing Trends, Analysis of Child Abuse and Neglect Research*, the *Civil Rights Directory*, and the *Conservation Yearbook*. Also done away with was *Selected U.S. Government Publications*, a free brochure that alerted readers to new items of general interest. The Government Printing Office instead invited the public to subscribe to another directory, published by a private firm, for $90 per year.

Although officials boasted about eliminating "waste," the claim was contested by many individuals and organizations. A librarian at the State University of New York at Albany conducted an informal survey in 1986 to assess the impact of the elimination of publications. She found that local service agencies and even the Albany office of the Small Business Administration refuted the government's depictions of the publications as superfluous. The county's 4-H program could no longer offer an auto safety course because of the elimination of low-cost materials previously available from Washington. The education program of a local health maintenance organization complained about the loss of publications about high blood pressure and prenatal care. A social service worker lamented the end of a series of booklets on daily living skills which she had used in work with the mentally retarded.

None of the groups had been consulted before the publications were taken out of print. Sara Knapp, who conducted the survey, concluded:

> Far from avoiding duplication of work, the gap left by abbreviating the federal publishing program has multiplied the work of local educators. . . . Apparently the Administration prefers flashy, short-term savings, even if it involves sacrificing information which could prevent problems. The more costly burden of remedying problems will, of course, fall on states and local communities.[13]

Federal statistical programs have also come under the OMB's knife. Government statistics expert Eleanor Chelimsky has written:

> Almost every major nondefense agency of the federal government has felt the effects of the administration's efforts to reduce its expenditures for data collection. . . . Even the tiny Statistical Policy Branch within the Office of Management and Budget,

which had the charge of coordinating and assuring the integrity of the federal government's highly decentralized statistical effort, [has] received the presidential order to cut or disband many of [its] data collection programs.[14]

Chelimsky estimated that some fifty-eight data series have been reduced or dropped entirely. Major budget cuts have inhibited statistical activity at the Census Bureau as well as numerous other agencies that cover areas like health, education, agriculture, and energy. Among other things, this trend has affected the planning and implementation of state and local services. Delays and less frequent analysis of statistics have distorted federal disbursements to states and individuals that are calculated according to federal numbers.

The private sector, ostensibly the beneficiary of the Reagan administration's efforts to scale back federal activities, has been one of the most vocal opponents of the cutbacks in the statistics area. Corporations traditionally have made extensive use of federal data on a wide range of subjects—demographic trends, economic conditions, labor force figures—in their business planning. The government's notion that private information vendors will fill in the gaps not only is dubious but also ignores the question of the integrity of the data. Noting that "the quality of the data gathered by most private organization is appalling," the chief economist of American Express said in 1982 that federal cutbacks in statistics would "increase the likelihood of business and government decisions based on erroneous information" and "cost the private and public sectors billions of dollars over the long run."[15]

No Information—No Problem!

Another consequence of the public cutbacks in government information is that they make it easier for the government to deny that problems exist, or to distort their nature. For example, the Reagan administration used dubious estimates of the number of homeless people to refute social workers and advocates for the homeless who were pointing to a growing national emergency. And a study conducted by the Department of Housing and Urban Development in 1984 denied that the number of homeless people was significant enough to merit federal involvement.[16]

In the same vein, President Reagan himself downplayed the problem of hunger and, indicating some sensitivity to the problem of public information, claimed that if hunger did exist in America, it was because poor people lacked knowledge about where to go for assistance. That such ignorance might have resulted from his own policies was not acknowledged.

The Big Sell-off

In its agenda for the second Reagan administration, the ultraconservative Heritage Foundation argued that privatization should be a "central theme" of the final Reagan years.[17] The administration agreed; it used every opportunity to push for the transfer of government programs to the private sector. Among the proposed targets for divestment have been the Coast Guard, the Tennessee Valley Authority, the health care system for veterans, and even federal prisons and the Postal Service. The government's share of Conrail was sold off in 1987.

Privatization is also an issue with regard to information. Declaring "war on waste," the princes of privatization have sought ways to transfer federal data collection, research, and publishing activities into the hands of profit-making companies. Since these private entities are not subject to federal rules regarding public access and are able to charge whatever the market will bear, privatization has the effect of further promoting government secrecy.

A government-wide plan to privatize information was formalized in 1985 with the issuance of OMB Circular A-130, entitled "Management of Federal Information Resources." Agencies were directed to explore possibilities of private-sector involvement before embarking on any new information programs.

In addition, agency responsibilities to provide information to the public were sharply limited through a definitional ploy that distinguished "access" programs—which agencies were by law required to provide—from "dissemination" programs, which were discretionary and therefore supposedly could be left to private firms.

Varied Responses from Industry

As we have noted, the industry response to privatization has not been entirely favorable. It was to be expected that those most enthusiastic would be the information vendors who view privatization as the opening of a new market, yet the nature of their objections to the new arrangement is intriguing. They advocate government withdrawal or "load shedding" only at the point where the function can be managed profitably; these same firms favor continuing government involvement in providing certain kinds of raw data that can later be privatized and turned into marketable products. For these firms, privatization means letting the private sector skim off the profitable aspects of data services while the government holds onto research and the other costly aspects of the process. Companies that are not sharing in this boondoggle are less likely to be cheerleaders for privatization.

Given this dynamic, it was therefore no surprise that the administration's effort in 1987 to privatize the National Technical Information Service generated a large volume of negative reaction from corporations as well as from educational and scientific organizations. The NTIS, started thirty years ago, disseminates material from a wide range of domestic and foreign sources and is supported entirely by user fees.

At a congressional hearing in 1987, John Shattuck of Harvard University listed a number of concerns relating to the privatization of NTIS. Among these were the end of the publication of those documents with low sales potential, because of the new profit motive; the probable loss of permanent, archival collections and of foreign research reports; a significant increase in the price of documents; and increased pressure to delete "sensitive" but unclassified information.[18]

The information industry, for its part, objected to total privatization, instead preferring that NTIS continue its traditional functions while the private sector concentrated on creating "value-added" services. Despite such opposition, the OMB tried to move ahead with its effort to privatize NTIS, but actions by Congress forced the agency to stop the implementation of its plan.

How much should a democratic government economize with regard to information it collects with taxpayer money? The OMB has shown little concern for the kind of serious problems raised by the process of privatization. In defense-related industries, it has long been federal policy to encourage the private development of technology originated with public funds. However, this idea has only recently been applied to government information. "Decisions have been made in the past to contract out part of an agency research program, but no one had ever thought of contracting out the entire operation because it was thought that basic control should be in government hands," says Bernadine Hoduski of the Joint Committee on Printing.

Once information is under private management, according to Hoduski, a particularly important consideration is ensuring that all citizens have access to it. In most cases of privatization sharp price increases take place. For instance, the annual government publication reporting decisions of the Merit Systems Protection Board, which oversees personnel practices in the federal government, cost $50; it was replaced with a private information service that charged subscribers $250 to $498.[19] In effect, the public pays twice: once for the original information and once for the features added by industry.

Ken Allen of the Information Industry Association, commenting on the future supply of information to depository libraries, has argued that the question of access should be directed at the government. "I think it would be unfair to place that burden on private publishers. If the government says that depository libraries are a safety net, which we in the industry agree with, the government should carry out its responsibility to finance the production of those documents."

Unfortunately, the OMB has done little to guarantee that agreements for privatizing or contracting out agency libraries include requirements for the continued preservation and dissemination of material. No provision has thus far been made to ensure public access to privatized material that would have been available under the Freedom of Information Act if it were still under agency supervision.

E. J. Josey, past president of the American Library Association, has stated:

> Nobody would deny the utility of many of these services provided by the private sector, but they are not available to all of the American people; their purpose is to yield a profit, and they are designed only for those who can pay for them. . . . Only the preservation of public services, publicly supported, can assure that each individual has equal and ready access to information.[20]

Libraries for Sale

Daniel Boorstin, former Librarian of Congress, has called libraries "the laboratory of our memory and the catalyst of our expectations." The spread of the privatization fever to these institutions has raised questions about their ability to continue serving in these roles.

In the past seven years, several federal agencies have turned over the management of their libraries to private firms. The libraries of the Department of Energy and even of the White House are now under private control. Aspen Systems, a subsidiary of a Dutch corporation, manages the library of the Department of Housing and Urban Development and in 1987 won a contract to operate the library of the National Oceanic and Atmospheric Administration (NOAA). (Turning over control to foreign entities raises additional problems concerning possible damage to national security interests. Ironically, the Reagan administration, which often pounded the drum of national security, did little to ensure that adequate monitoring mechanisms were written into contracts with firms from abroad.)

Contracting out federal libraries jeopardizes priceless data and archival material through the withdrawal of professional librarians and the introduction of profit motives, which have little to do with preserving the public memory. Testifying before a Senate subcommittee in December 1987, Eileen D. Cooke of the American Library Association revealed that the contractor planning to take over management of the NOAA library planned to fulfill the promise of reduced costs through partial use of volunteers in the place of professional staff. Cooke noted that the use of unqualified personnel could jeopardize the integrity of the facility and criticized the OMB for ignoring the "hidden costs of contracting."[21]

In 1986 it was reported that the price for purchasing government information had soared at federal agencies, including the National Library of Medicine and the Department of Agriculture, where private firms were contracted to computerize information.[22]

Public libraries also face dangers from the privatization of government information. As a public institution funded by tax dollars, the public library traditionally has made its services available to the community free of charge. As the prices of government publications and other materials increase, this tradition of free and equal-opportunity access to library information is in jeopardy.

Depository libraries, which provide access to federal publications, have been crippled by the refusal of Congress to appropriate funds that would allow them to obtain and make accessible the large number of government documents available only in computerized form.[23] The Congressional Joint Committee on Printing has recommended that a pilot study be conducted to consider delivering government material to the libraries in electronic format, a project the Committee estimates will cost some $800,000. Congress delayed its approval of this expenditure, even though it allocated $1 million in the 1988 budget so that its own committees could receive documents indexed and then sold back to the government by Westlaw, Congressional Quarterly, and other private companies. This inequity ensures that the elected—but not their constituencies—will remain informed.

Computers and Censorship

The ever-growing use of computers to store, process, and disseminate information raises a number of other important issues regarding public access and general political freedom.[24]

A recent example is the OMB's plan to compile a computerized master list of individuals who have in some way failed to comply with government regulations and to prevent them from receiving federal loans and other benefits (other than personal entitlements such as Social Security). As with paperwork reduction, the OMB has taken a seemingly acceptable notion—preventing people who defraud the government in one area from receiving benefits in another—and created a mechanism that undermines constitutional rights.

The sweeping extent of the OMB's plan—which was implemented in 1988—turned the master list into a potential blacklist. The fear among civil libertarians is that it could also be extended to punish a variety of Americans who express any disagreement with government policy. Among the grounds for exclusion from government benefits and contracts are engaging in "seriously improper" conduct or showing a lack of "business integrity"; performing poorly on any grant from a public agency; or doing business with others whom one "reasonably should have known" were in violation of federal law.[25]

123

These vaguely worded criteria seem to leave the door wide open for arbitrary and punitive action. Congressman Jack Brooks objected that the list "offends many of the basic precepts upon which this nation is founded" and introduces the computer-programmed presumption of guilt by association. Gary Bass, director of OMB Watch, described it as "a hit list" that could be dangerous for individuals and organizations that voiced criticisms of government policies, or anyone who simply fell out of favor with a particular agency."[26]

Proponents of privatization also ignore the fact that private companies can use computers to restrict access. In 1987 Dialog Information Services, a leading provider of on-line information, barred a group of its subscribers from gaining access to financial data about certain companies collected by Dun & Bradstreet. Those prevented from obtaining information included the Communications Workers of America, the American Federation of State, County and Municipal Employees, and other unions.

Moreover, the government may attempt to extend its censorship policies to privately owned databases, as it did in 1984 after the president signed National Security Decision Directive 145, "National Policy on Telecommunications and Automated Information Systems Security." As noted earlier, this directive called for limiting unclassified information that is sold commercially; the rationale for restricting private sources was that unclassified data available in commercial databases could be pieced together like a mosaic that, when taken in the aggregate, revealed highly classified information.[27] (For more on this issue, see chapter 7.)

The Most Critical Resource

Providing access to information is a major part of maintaining democratic values and ensuring that people can play a meaningful role in political decision-making. The price society pays for failure to remove restrictions on information is an apathetic, ill-informed, and vulnerable citizenry.

In a democratic society, the most crucial function of information is to provide the basis for critical thought needed to hold the line against the suppression of civil liberties. Recent policies have caused severe reductions in the information available about many vital issues through paperwork reduction, deregulation of industry, and the Information Collection Budget. Freed of bureaucratic jargon, these policies emerge as powerful new indirect techniques for limiting public participation in government.

In the words of Thomas Jefferson: "If a nation expects to be ignorant and free in a state of civilization, it expects what never was and never will be. . . . If we are to guard against ignorance and remain free, it is the responsibility of every American to be informed."

Notes

1. Quoted in Mark A. Pinsky, "OMB's Chokehold on Government," *The Nation*, 23 January 1988.

2. Administrative Procedure Act, 5 U.S.C. 551–559, 701–706.

3. 5 U.S.C. 552 (a)(1) and (a)(2).

4. David Stockman, *The Triumph of Politics* (New York: Harper & Row, 1986), p. 8. Stockman writes that the Reagan revolution "defied all of the overwhelming forces, interests, and impulses of American democracy."

5. Executive Order 12291, issued 17 February 1981; Executive Order 12498, issued 4 January 1985.

6. OMB Watch, *Eye on Paperwork* (Washington, DC: OMB Watch, October 1986), p. 10. A study by a public interest group later reported that contaminants were found in nearly one-fifth of the country's public water systems. See "Study of Drinking Water Assails EPA as Derelict in Monitoring," *The New York Times*, 5 January 1988.

7. More about the dynamics of agency proceedings, including the OMB's interventions, can be found in *Through the Corridors of Power: A Guide to Federal Rulemaking* (Washington: OMB Watch, 1987).

8. Unlike the national budget, the Information Collection Budget is not reviewed by Congress.

9. Environmental Defense Fund v. EPA, 449 U.S. 1112 (1988).

10. 5 U.S.C. 552 (a)(2).

11. A study by the General Accounting Office in 1985 for the House Committee on Government Operations found that many agencies did not publish required material, provided erroneous information, or were otherwise not in compliance with FOIA's disclosure provisions. "Freedom of Information Act, Noncompliance with Affirmative Disclosure Provisions" (GAO GGD-86-68), April 1986.

12. It did not help matters when the IRS proposed to restrict advocacy by nonprofit (501[c][3]) organizations by redefining much of it as lobbying (OMB Watch Memorandum, 6 February 1987).

125

13. Sara D. Knapp, "OMB A-130, A Policy Which Could Affect Your Reference Service," *The Reference Librarian*, February 1988. This fine article also analyzes other consequences of recent changes in government information policy.

14. Eleanor Chelimsky, "Budget Cuts, Data and Evaluation," *Social Science and Public Policy*, March/April 1985.

15. Quoted in Ann Crittenden, "A World with Fewer Numbers," *The New York Times*, 11 July 1982.

16. "Body Count: How the Reagan Administration Hides the Homeless," *The Village Voice*, 3 December 1985.

17. The Heritage Foundation, *Mandate for Leadership II: Continuing the Conservative Revolution* (Washington, DC: The Heritage Foundation, 1984).

18. Statement of John Shattuck, Vice-President for Government, Community and Public Affairs, Harvard University, on behalf of the Association of American Universities and the Association of Research Libraries, House Subcommittee on Science, Research and Technology, 14 July 1987.

19. Nancy C. Kranich, "Changing Government Information Policy," paper delivered at the 1986 annual meeting of the Organization of American Historians and the National Council on Public History, p. 4.

20. Statement of E. J. Josey before the Postsecondary Education Subcommittee, House Committee on Education and Labor, 8 April 1986. See also Anita R. Schiller and Herbert I. Schiller, "Commercializing Information," *The Nation*, 4 October 1986.

21. Prepared statement of Eileen D. Cooke, Associate Executive Director of the American Library Association, before the Subcommittee on Federal Services, Post Office and Civil Service of the Senate Committee on Governmental Affairs, 17 December 1987.

22. "Computerizing Uncle Sam's Data: Oh, How the Public is Paying," *Business Week*, 15 December 1986.

23. Joint Committee on Printing (Report of), *Provision of Federal Government Publications in Electronic Format to Depository Libraries*, Washington, DC: GPO, 1984.

24. A valuable report on this subject is *Technology and U.S. Government Information Policies: Catalysts for New Partnerships*, (Washington, DC: Association of Research Libraries, 1987).

25. Martin Tolchin, "U.S. Plans to Make a Master List of Abusers of Aid Programs," *The New York Times*, 23 December 1987; "Guidelines for Nonprocurement, Debarment and Suspension," *Federal Register*, 29 May 1987. See also Francis J. Flaherty, "The Feds Prepare a Blacklist," *The Progressive*, February 1988.

26. Tolchin, "U.S. Plans to Make a Master List."

27. For more about restrictions put on commercial vendors, see Nancy Kranich, "Government Information: Less is Dangerous," *Thought and Action: The NEA Higher Education Journal*, March 1988.

Selected Readings

American Library Association. *Less Access to Less Information By and About the U.S. Government* (a chronology). Washington, DC: ALA, 1982–1988.

Demac, Donna. "The Budget and Beyond," chapter 3 of *Keeping American Uniformed: Government Secrecy in the 1980s.* New York: Pilgrim, 1984.

Durrance, Joan. *Armed for Action: Library Response to Citizen Information Needs.* New York: Neal-Schuman, 1984.

Federal Library and Information Center Committee. *Federal Information Policies, Views of a Concerned Community: Fourth Annual Forum, Summary of Proceedings.* Washington, DC: Library of Congress, 1987.

Hernon, Peter, and C. R. McClure. *Federal Information Policies in the 1980s: Conflicts and Issues.* Norwood, NJ: Ablex, 1987.

Marwick, Christine. *Your Right to Government Information.* ACLU Handbook. New York: Bantam, 1985.

Morgan, David. *The Flacks of Washington: Government Information and the Public Agenda.* Westport, CT: Greenwood, 1986.

Mosco, Vincent, and Janet Wasko. *The Political Economy of Information.* Madison: University of Wisconsin Press, 1988.

OMB Watch. *OMB Control of Government Publications: Review and Elimination.* Washington, DC: OMB Watch 1986.

OMB Watch. *Through the Corridors of Power: A Guide to Federal Rulemaking.* Washington, DC: OMB Watch, 1987.

People for the American Way. *Government Secrecy: Decisions Without Democracy.* Washington, DC: People for the American Way, 1987.

9

MANAGING THE NEWS AND VIEWS

Government Controls on Media and Travel

*If there is any fixed star in our constitutional constella-
tion, it is that no official, high or petty, can prescribe what
shall be orthodox in politics, nationalism, religion or other
matters of opinion or force citizens to confess by word or act
their faith therein.*[1]

Freedom of expression in the United States since colonial times
has been understood as freedom from fear of government persecution for personal values and beliefs. The First Amendment
reflects a deep commitment to individual expression, including
the right of citizens to form associations with others. At the same
time, a robust press that delves freely into the dark and embarrassing corners of government has always been an essential
feature of American democracy. Its job is to "serve the governed,
not the governors" through constant scrutiny of official conduct.
In addition, the press has often served the purpose of providing
public visibility for the diverse ideas and activities of people
outside the mainstream.

Throughout the course of U.S. history these functions have
often been suppressed by federal and local governments, especially during periods of social upheaval. Editors were persecuted
under the Sedition Acts of 1798; publisher Elijah Lovejoy of
Illinois was killed by an angry mob for opposing slavery; local
officials brought major libel suits against newspapers to discourage coverage of the civil rights movement in the 1960s.

During the last decade, the major challenges to freedom of the
press have entailed government restrictions based on the need to
protect "national security." And although no American government ever has existed that did not keep secrets or resent the press

for asking questions at what it considered to be inopportune moments, the Reagan and Bush administrations have been remarkable in their systematic efforts to control public views on important issues, including their relentless efforts to restrict coverage by news organizations.

The U.S. government has resorted to a variety of dubious practices in order to escape public scrutiny, including "black" (secret) budget items, the classification or destruction of sensitive documents, covert operations, and outright lying. By the same token, what is out in the open is often presented through the filter of public relations.

However inevitable it might be in the world of commerce, public relations in the political arena is a pernicious force. Staged events, disinformation, propaganda, carefully crafted White Papers that seek to attract support for government domestic and foreign policies, and other such practices facilitate deception or, at best, the selective disclosure of truth. To these the Reagan administration added such policies as restrictions on foreign travel by Americans and on visits by certain foreigners to this country—both of which sought to close minds by closing borders. The overall impact was that, in the words of James Reston, "nothing is lost but the honest cut and thrust of democracy."[2]

The War Against Subversion

Although government relations with the press and with dissidents have been in tension since the beginning of the Republic, it was not until the early twentieth century that the government made concerted attempts to control public opinion. The end of America's isolation in the world, the fear of war, and the rise of radicalism at home and abroad all worked to create a climate of repression. Before World War I laws were passed that called for the deportation of immigrants who held anarchist views. In 1917, less than two weeks after the United States entered the war, President Wilson created the Committee on Public Information as a vehicle for government control of the press and named journalist George Creel to head it.

The Creel Committee, as it came to be known, blazed a new trail in disseminating government propaganda and enforcing press censorship. Using an army of journalists, academics, and members of the clergy, Creel stoked the fires of patriotism and encouraged emotional attacks against the Germans. Newspapers were intimidated into publishing only information approved by the government and were expected to join in the national xenophobia.

In the end, the hysteria was directed as much against supposed domestic enemies as it was against America's foreign foes. Creel's efforts reinforced the already existing campaign against radicals and labor militants, and public outrage converged in an all-out attack on those who opposed America's entry into the war. Antiwar activists were rounded up, and hundreds, including Eugene Debs, were imprisoned. Pacifists were beaten and tortured. The persecution of dissidents continued even after the end of the war, and in the early 1920s the Red Scare reached its climax with the infamous Palmer Raids, in which thousands of people were imprisoned and many were deported.

These unsavory episodes left a bitter residue, and the next time the federal government felt the need to manage public opinion on a broad scale, those in power saw to it that somewhat more benign practices were adopted. Franklin Roosevelt set a new tone with his famous fireside chats in the 1930s. In the early stages of World War II, Roosevelt moved cautiously in trying to win the public over to the idea of U.S. intervention. Before the attack on Pearl Harbor, according to historian Richard Steele, Roosevelt had been engaged in a three-year attempt to mobilize public sentiment. One of the approaches his advisers had suggested called for the creation of local defense committees that would get people involved in "propaganda of the act." Fearing censure by both the press and Congress, Roosevelt vetoed the idea, observing that it depended too much on a "good ballyhoo artist and speech maker."[3]

Once war was declared in 1941, a code of wartime practices for newspapers and other periodicals was issued by the newly created Office of Censorship, which set forth categories of news that could not be published without government authorization. Included in this list was information on troop strength and air attacks, and photographs that might be useful to the enemy. The war years saw few instances of conflict between the Office of Censorship and the press, and the high level of public support for the war that accounted for this gave propaganda and censorship unprecedented legitimacy.

Even before the war ended, the stage had been set for the conflict to come. The origins of a new attack on dissident views lay in the creation in 1938 of a House Committee, headed by Representative Martin Dies, to investigate "un-American" activities. The Dies Committee originally drew wide support from groups that believed it would focus on Nazi activities in the United States. But Dies directed much of his attack against the left, which, for him and his colleagues, included the labor movement and the Roosevelt administration.

Wartime exigencies took precedence over the Dies campaign, but after the conflicts in Europe and Asia ended, the ideological battle at home resumed, led first by the House Un-American Activities Committee and then by Senator Joseph McCarthy. The new campaign included attacks on alleged subversion in the film industry, television, the academic world, and government agencies, including the State Department.

Amid such crusades, the First Amendment lost much of its force. The Smith Act and the McCarran-Walter Act made membership in communist organizations, classroom instruction on "subversive" subjects, and other forms of dissident speech and association grounds for prosecution and imprisonment. In 1951 President Truman issued Executive Order 10290, which gave all executive branch agencies the power to classify information. Robert McLean, president of the Associated Press at the time, said the order invited "a creeping censorship of a kind never before established in time of peace or even in time of war."[4]

Self-Censorship and National Security

By the 1960s the Red Scare had died down, but the Cold War was still very much alive. The federal government kept up pressure on the news media, and editors were usually inclined to cooperate. The willingness of *The New York Times* and other papers to accede to President Kennedy's request to delay reporting the Bay of Pigs invasion in Cuba showed the degree to which the press had been persuaded to be "responsible."

Some of the mainstream media became deeply invested in such camaraderie. By the mid-1960s, official statements were laced with partial truths in efforts to minimize the extent of political disruptions at home and abroad. Kennedy's press secretary went so far as to state publicly that the president had a right to lie under certain circumstances.

Edward R. Murrow, once the nation's most respected journalist, took on the job of propagandist by agreeing to head the United States Information Agency (USIA). Whatever his private reservations, he was willing to justify the government's position on propaganda before Congress in 1963, testifying that: "no computer clicks, no cash register rings when a man changes his mind or opts for freedom. . . . [Nonetheless,] our arsenal of persuasion must be as ready as our nuclear arsenal, and used as never before."[5]

Even if no computer clicked, the government was committing itself more deeply to schemes aimed at the outright engineering of public opinion. During the war in Vietnam, first Lyndon Johnson and then Richard Nixon compromised the integrity and the stature of the White House with policies built around deception.

Throughout most of the 1960s, the mainstream press dutifully reported official statements as fact; in time, it found itself running behind the better-informed sectors of the American public, many of whom turned increasingly to alternate media to obtain their news. Some journalists actually worked secretly in the employ of the government. In November 1973 the *Washington Star-News* reported that the CIA had thirty-six journalists on its payroll. The news prompted Stuart Loory to conduct an investigation, which revealed that the CIA had contracts with dozens of journalists who worked overseas as stringers, free-lance writers, and full-time correspondents.[6]

Not long after this, the Senate Select Committee on Intelligence (the Church Committee) found evidence that more than two hundred wire services, newspapers, magazines, and book publishing companies were owned outright by the CIA. In 1977, articles by former *Washington Post* investigative reporter Carl Bernstein and by *New York Times* reporters uncovered additional evidence of links between intelligence agencies and the media, both inside and outside the United States.[7]

Daniel Ellsberg's Hot Potato

The ground rules of government relations with the press briefly became the subject of heated public controversy when, in 1971, the government moved to prevent publication of papers on the history of the Vietnam War that had been circulated by a disaffected intelligence analyst, Daniel Ellsberg. On application of the government, courts in New York and Washington issued orders to halt publication of the "Pentagon Papers," as they came to be known. It was the first time in American history that the press had been restrained from publishing news on foreign policy on the grounds that publication would threaten national security.

The public sentiment regarding these cases was impassioned and, to a large extent, ill informed. After almost two hundred years, the government and a great number of Americans still did not understand how the freewheeling give-and-take between reporters and government officials could benefit the workings of a democracy.

In an important affidavit, Max Frankel, then the Washington bureau chief of *The New York Times*, tried to explain the underlying issue:

> I know how strange this must sound. We have been taught, particularly in the past generation of spy scares and the Cold War, to think of secrets as secrets. . . . This is [now] an antiquated, quaint and romantic view. For practically everything that our Government does, plans, thinks, hears and contemplates in the realms of foreign policy is stamped and treated as secret—and then unraveled by the same Government, by the Congress and by the press in one continuing round of professional and social contacts and cooperative and competitive exchanges of information. . . . The Government hides what it can—and the press pries out what it can. . . . Each side in this "game" regularly "wins" and "loses" a round or two.[8]

In light of the prevailing confusion, the Supreme Court's ruling in the Pentagon Papers case—that the government had failed to justify its claim of prior restraint—was of major significance. Nevertheless, it is doubtful whether this historic decision did much to alter the perception of those Americans who blamed the media for being unpatriotic. Nor did the decision do much to embolden the press. Some observers argued that just the opposite was true—that even in the wake of their victory, editors scrambled to show their patriotic credentials.

Further evidence that the press corps was skittish about government complaints emerged in 1976, when CBS reporter Daniel Schorr gave *The Village Voice* a copy of the House Intelligence Committee's report (the Pike Report) on CIA misconduct, which Congress had voted to keep secret. Schorr believed that his obligation as a journalist was to assist publication, but many of his colleagues disagreed. As Congress launched an investigation, Schorr was fired by CBS and became the subject of widespread criticism in both the broadcast and print media.[9]

The issue of just how far the press should go in accommodating the government was becoming increasingly serious. In 1979, *The Progressive* magazine was about to publish an article on the H-bomb that was based entirely on information previously made public. Nonetheless, the federal government was able to obtain a court order restraining publication. The court's willingness to accept the government's allegations that the article would endanger the national security—without requiring proof, as required just a few years earlier in the Pentagon Papers case—was an ominous indication of how greatly judicial safeguards against press censorship had declined.

The Constitution Gets "Snepped"

This concern was reinforced by court decisions that upheld the use of nondisclosure contracts as a means of controlling the speech of government employees. For years intelligence agency personnel had been required to sign agreements obligating them not to share secret information and to submit their speeches, articles, and other writings for review prior to publication. In 1974, the government relied on such a contract to force the deletion of a large portion of a book, *The CIA and The Cult of Intelligence*, writen by John Marks and former CIA agent Victor Marchetti.

Several years later, the possibility of relying on similar contracts but on a wider basis was raised in a Supreme Court decision. The case involved a government suit against a former CIA agent, Frank Snepp, who had failed to submit a book manuscript for prior review as was stipulated in his contract. Both sides agreed that Snepp's book, *Decent Interval*, contained no classified information. But the Supreme Court accepted the government's claim that it had an unconditional right to review the manuscript, and it also agreed that the government had the right to confiscate all the author's proceeds from the book.[10]

Even more significant was a statement, contained in a footnote to the Snepp decision, indicating that the Court approved of the government's use of employment contracts with "national security" provisions to restrict First Amendment rights. The implications of the Court's endorsement were unclear, yet it was so troublesome that then Attorney General Benjamin Civiletti immediately adopted guidelines to limit its application. Within a few years, however, the full impact of the *Snepp* decision became apparent as the Reagan administration used it as the primary justification for new restrictions on the speech and writings of hundreds of thousands of government employees (see chapter 7).

The Communications Specialists

As the most skillful practitioner of executive branch public relations in American history, the Reagan administration provided a grave lesson in the types of government controls that can be used to narrow the range of public discourse.

The administration's program to control the press and public opinion consisted of four main elements: a broad effort to reduce the amount and the quality of information available to the public; the mounting of elaborately orchestrated news events and photo opportunities; continual public criticism of the news media; and, perhaps most important, a skillful campaign to separate and insulate the president from the consequences of his own policies.

From the outset, the administration treated all those who did not embrace its programs as an alien force. *The Nation* magazine wryly captured this in the statement: "The Reagan Administration's faith in the miracle of the free marketplace has never extended to the marketplace of ideas. There are no supplysiders among the Reaganites when it comes to the First Amendment."[11]

Providing access to the facts was not what the administration was about, which accounted for much of its open hostility toward the press. Indeed, the early 1980s was a golden age for the ballyhoo official. The era was typified by a series of less than convincing official reports that claimed to show, for example, that hunger and homelessness were not major social problems in America.

In 1981, when the administration's saber-rattling in Central America generated widespread public opposition, the State Department issued a White Paper, "Communist Interference in El Salvador," purporting to present "definitive evidence" of

Soviet military support to overthrow the government of El Salvador. Before long it was widely challenged as inaccurate, at best, and the State Department allowed that it could not substantiate many of the "report's" claims.

On occasion, the Reagan White House produced dubiously motivated human witnesses to corroborate its official positions, as in early 1988, when a former Sandinista cabinet officer testified about the repressive practices and the allegedly dangerous Soviet connections of the Sandinista government just at the time Congress was preparing for a crucial vote on aid to the contras.[12]

Regulating the Press

While he was press spokesman for the Reagan administration, Larry Speakes kept a sign on his desk that read: "You don't tell us how to stage the news and we don't tell you how to cover it." In fact, the White House has devoted extraordinary energy to both orchestrating official events and influencing the way in which the media report on them.[13]

According to *New York Times* White House correspondent Steve Weisman, Reagan and his aides "achieved a new level of control over the mechanics of modern communication—the staging of news events for maximum press coverage, the timing of announcements to hit the largest television audiences."[14]

The press's access to the president also was more controlled than during any previous administration. The White House initiated a policy of holding daily meetings to determine the official line of the day, which was intended to cover the president's image as well as pending issues. This approved version of the issues of the day was then sent out to press spokesmen throughout the rest of the federal government. In addition, agency personnel were given strict orders to report all contacts with the media. By the mid-1980s, the administration had put into place regulations that subjected thousands of agency employees to criminal prosecution for disclosing information without authorization.

All this was part of a deliberate attempt to change the ground rules and practices of press access. President Reagan and his advisers not only believed that the media were hostile but also were convinced that their ideal of the corporate state required greatly tightened control over the information that reached the public.

The administration's plans in this regard might have encountered serious barriers if the public had been able to recognize the continuing official criticism of the media as a calculated plan to neutralize press criticism and create an aura of benevolent authority. But the president and his press representatives successfully headed off opposition with frequent and ostensibly good-natured statements that accused news organizations of having little concern for their readers and viewers, and of creating rather than reporting the news.

This strategy enjoyed enormous success, especially in the administration's early years. Even the press was ambivalent about whether or not to call attention to the administration's efforts to disarm the American public by discrediting its pipeline to information. Some journalists wrote articles on the subject for limited-circulation magazines, but very few took the message to the larger public. The White House let it be known that it intended to be militant about reprimanding large media organizations whose coverage extended beyond its idea of accurate reporting.

In a 1984 article in *The Village Voice*, Reporter Mark Hertsgaard tried to account for the reticence of the press as misplaced concern on the part of reporters and editors over the issue of appearing to take sides:

> It is precisely this philosophy—WE DON'T TAKE SIDES—that has shaped coverage not just of Reagan's Central America speech but of his entire presidency. Reluctant to present too negative a picture of the president for fear of appearing partisan, and willing to believe that neutrality is truth and accuracy is bias, the news media made the Reagan Administration's work much easier by becoming an active participant in its own manipulation.[15]

By not taking the offensive, the press almost guaranteed that the administration would succeed in efforts to align itself with the public against the media. This dynamic could certainly be seen when newsmen were kept out of the island of Grenada during the first three days of the U.S. invasion there in 1983. This single episode soon led to new, more permanent restrictions on the press during other overseas military activities. As the use of press pools became more entrenched as an acceptable entity to press organizations, the public could no longer count on having individual news accounts that were not managed in some way by Pentagon officials. To the disadvantage of all, reporters continued to find themselves excluded during the most significant moments of military activity.[16]

The press has hardly been blameless in these matters. In their eagerness to maintain access, reporters have consented to let the lead and the subsequent content of their stories be dictated to them by senior pool representatives. Another of the mistakes press organizations made was to believe that compromises reached on a limited number of issues would allow the press and the government to develop more cooperative relations. But there were signs from the very beginning of the Reagan years that the administration's agenda was more sweeping.

A 1982 executive order established new standards for the classification of information, instructing agencies: "When in doubt classify." The order also removed the earlier requirement that agencies balance the government's secrecy-related interest against the public interest in the requested information and, for the first time, allowed the reclassification of information (see chapter 7). Moreover, the president was quick to issue a new executive order giving intelligence agencies authority to wiretap and search newsrooms.

By 1985 press pools, secrecy contracts, and the "line of the day" were firmly in place, and the administration's appetite for control remained unsated. Moreover, new curbs had been imposed by Congress, including still more categories of information to be exempted from release under the Freedom of Information Act, and a law that made it a crime to publish the names of intelligence agents.[17] A plan was also in process to establish an American equivalent of the British Official Secrets Act, by making the publication of classified information a criminal offense. Toward this end, the administration moved against a civilian Navy employee, Samuel Loring Morison (see chapter 7).

At the time of Morison's conviction in 1985, writer David Wise observed that the case had been part of a two-pronged strategy "to intimidate officials for unauthorized leaks at one end and intimidate reporters at the other end."[18]

Patrolling the Ideological Border

The Reagan administration's efforts to confine the parameters of public debate included restrictions on information flowing across our borders in both directions. In 1983, relying on regulations that allowed the government to deny films duty-free certification if they lacked "adequate American points of reference," the USIA refused to grant a permit for the export of *The Killing Ground*, an ABC documentary about toxic waste, claiming that the film "would mislead a foreign audience into believing that the American public needed arousing to the dangers of hazardous wastes when this is no longer the case."

During the next several years, certification was denied to dozens of films on such topics as teenage drug use and the dangers of uranium mining. Though films denied certification could still be distributed abroad, their makers could no longer qualify for the usual exemptions from paying taxes and duties in other countries.[19] In 1987 a federal court ruled that the criteria the government was using to grant and deny duty-free export status were unconstitutional. Shortly thereafter, new rules were issued, but they did little to lessen the danger of indirect censorship, since they allowed films to be labeled as "propaganda" if they did not offer an acceptable range of opinion on controversial subjects and did not present topics in what was determined to be a "primarily factual manner." According to attorney David Cole, who represented a group of independent filmmakers in a suit that challenged the new regulations, "essentially what they're saying is that unless you put out a view of America that is absolutely Ronald Reagan rosy clean, they're going to say it's propaganda."[20]

The USIA also restricted the entry of dozens of films into the United States by refusing to approve them as fit for educational or other use. For example, three films produced by the National Film Board of Canada on the perils of nuclear war and acid rain were labeled as "political propaganda."[21]

The administration's political litmus test also extended to other areas. In 1984 it was discovered that the USIA was keeping a blacklist of people whose views rendered them undesirable for overseas speaking tours. Walter Cronkite, Coretta Scott King, and Gary Hart were among those the agency believed could not be trusted.

The Reagan administration's move away from the free exchange of ideas and information was also visible in its attempts to control travel. Restrictions on the right to travel are justly denounced by conservatives in their critiques of the policies of the Soviet Union, yet similar curbs have been placed both on American citizens and on foreigners trying to visit the United States.

In the first instance, two Supreme Court decisions of the 1980s have greatly expanded the government's authority to limit foreign travel. In one case, filed during the Carter administration, the Court held that the secretary of state could revoke the passport of former CIA agent Philip Agee, an outspoken critic of intelligence agency abuses and a writer who, according to the government, was guilty of exposing the identity of CIA officers and agents. The broader meaning of the Court's ruling was that the freedom of American citizens to travel was subordinate to the needs of national security and foreign policy.[22]

The second Court decision upheld regulations that established criminal penalties for Americans traveling in certain countries. At issue were rules requiring people (other than journalists and academics doing research) to apply for licenses in order to travel to Cuba. According to the Reagan administration, these regulations were necessary to ensure that money spent by Americans in Cuba would not be used to finance subversion in Central America. In 1987, on the same grounds, the American Psychological Association was denied an exemption to attend the InterAmerican Congress of Psychology in Cuba. It now appears that most U.S. citizens cannot travel to Cuba, and that they may be prevented from going elsewhere if the government decides that it would endanger the national interest.[23]

The curbs on travel by foreigners were based on the 1952 Immigration and Nationality Act, better known as the McCarran-Walter Act. The law, passed during the McCarthy era, established a long list of reasons for which foreigners could be denied visas to visit the United States. The most serious of these had ideological grounds: Those who were deemed excludable included anyone who had been a member of a communist or anarchist organization, who had written materials advocating such views, or "whose activities would be contrary to the public interest."

Over the following three decades the law was used to exclude countless foreigners, including Belgian Marxist economist Ernest

Mandel, French radical theoretician Regis Debray, and such Latin American literary figures as Gabriel García Márquez, Carlos Fuentes, and Julio Cortázar, among many others. In 1972 the Supreme Court upheld the law, saying that the "plenary government power to make policies and rules for the exclusion of aliens" outweighed the First Amendment rights of U.S. citizens to hear what the foreigners had to say.

The Reagan administration used the law extensively. In 1982 it withheld visas from some five hundred people from around the world who planned to attend a special session on disarmament at the United Nations. In the following years the "undesirables" kept out of the country have included Italian playwright Dario Fo and actress Franca Rame, Nicaraguan interior minister Tomas Borge, Canadian naturalist and author Farley Mowat, and Hortensia de Allende, widow of the slain Chilean leader.

The law was sometimes used against those who already had visas. In 1986, when Colombian journalist Patricia Lara arrived at Kennedy Airport in New York to attend an awards dinner at Columbia University, she was taken into custody. Although her papers were in order, Lara's name had appeared on an Immigration and Naturalization Service (INS) list of some 40,000 people suspected of "subversive, Communist or terrorist activities." She was jailed for five days and then deported.

Another case concerned the American-born writer Margaret Randall, a critic of American government policies who had lived abroad for many years and had relinquished her American citizenship. In 1984 she returned to the United States to be near her elderly parents and to teach at the University of New Mexico. Using the McCarran-Walter Act, the INS denied her application for permanent residency and moved to deport her—clearly because of her political views; she had written widely in support of the Cuban revolution and had lived in Cuba.

Working with the Center for Constitutional Rights and receiving support from groups including PEN American Center, Randall challenged the INS. After five years of litigation, her problems appeared to end in 1989 as McCarran-Walter began to crumble. The Supreme Court let stand a lower court order limiting the power of the administration to exclude aliens for ideological reasons. Then Congress passed a two-year ban on the ideological exclusion for temporary visitors but retained it for those seeking permanent residence. Until McCarran-

Walter is completely and finally abolished, the danger of ideological control remains, especially for those who are not well known and thus less able to avoid the stigma attached to being excluded as political "undesirables."[24]

The Reagan administration's preoccupation with controlling foreign opinion was perhaps clearest in the initiative known as Project Democracy. The asserted aim of the program was to promote American values abroad. In fact, the broader agenda was to counter widespread criticism of U.S. military and foreign policies in Europe.

Operating under the auspices of a group called the National Endowment for Democracy, the project represented a continuation of the foreign propaganda efforts carried out by the U.S. government since the end of World War II. But while such previous initiatives were taken directly by federal agencies, such as the USIA—which remained active and was involved in new projects like the Worldnet satellite channel—Project Democracy was to be implemented by private groups, including the U.S. Chamber of Commerce, the AFL-CIO, and other organizations known for their anticommunist ideology. It was later made known that a large percentage of the funds for the project, which were appropriated by Congress only after the CIA promised that it would not be involved, ended up in the hands of foreign political parties, labor unions, and publishers who were friendly to the administration. Another issue that has been raised concerns possible links between the aboveground Project Democracy and the covert network of the same name overseen by Oliver North. The Tower Commission reported that it could find no evidence linking the two organizations, but it seems that the full story has yet to be told.[25]

A democratic society must afford opportunities for the expression of a wide variety of political, religious, and social values. The Bill of Rights exists because its authors were determined to prevent the government from regulating the expression of American citizens.

As we begin to emerge from a period in which both individual rights of expression and freedom of the press have been weakened by a multitude of regulations and by the remarkably successful public relations initiatives of the Reagan administration, we must recognize how narrow we have allowed the field for free expression to become. Once in place, such policies tend to become entrenched and to produce self-censorship. We must be on guard against "the gradual and silent encroachments of those in power" that James Madison warned about, for these encroachments, none too silent in recent years, are today perhaps the gravest in the history of the Republic.[26]

Notes

1. West Virginia State Board of Education v. Barnette, 319 U.S. 624 (1943).

2. James Reston, "Reagan Beats the Press," *The New York Times,* 4 November 1984.

3. Richard Steele, "Preparing the Public for War: Efforts to Establish a National Propaganda Agency, 1940–41," *American Historical Review* 75, no. 7 (1970) p. 1640.

4. Cited in Walter Brasch and Dana Ulloth, eds., *The Press and the State.* Lanham, MD: University Press of America, 1986, p. 399.

5. Statement by Edward R. Murrow, Director of the USIA, before the Subcommittee on International Organizations and Movements of the Committee on Foreign Affairs, House of Representatives, 28 March 1963. See Theodore Sorensen, *The Word War* (New York: Harper & Row, 1968).

6. "The CIA's Use of the Press—A Mighty Wurlitzer," *Columbia Journalism Review,* September/October 1974.

7. Carl Bernstein, "The CIA and the Media," *Rolling Stone,* 20 October 1977; and a series of articles on the CIA and public opinion in *The New York Times,* 25–27 December 1977.

8. The Frankel affidavit can be found in David Wise, *Politics of Lying* (New York: Random House, 1973), pp. 105–106.

9. Daniel Schorr, *Clearing the Air* (Boston: Houghton Mifflin, 1977).

10. Snepp v. U.S., 444 U.S. 507 (1980).

11. "Why Johnny Can't Speak," *The Nation,* 30 January 1988.

12. Alexander Cockburn, "Beat the Devil," *The Nation,* 26 December 1987, 2 January 1988; Joe Pichirallo, "U.S. Capitalizes on a Defection: Nicaraguan's 'Betrayal' Helps to Make Case for Contras," *The Washington Post,* 8 January 1988.

13. See *The Reagan Administration and The News Media,* a summary of more than 130 actions taken to restrict the media, prepared by the Reporters Committee on Freedom of the Press.

14. Steve Weisman, "The President and the Press," *The New York Times Magazine,* 14 October 1984.

15. Mark Hertsgaard, "How Reagan Seduced Us," *The Village Voice,* 18 September 1984.

16. For example, "Gathering News in the Persian Gulf," *The New York Times*, 4 January 1988, recounts how Pentagon officials denied reporters who had been selected for a press pool access to important moments of a military excursion.

17. Intelligence Identities Protection Act. P.L. 97-200, 96 Stat. 122 50 U.S.C.A., 421–426.

18. Quoted in Dom Bonafede, "Muzzling the Media," *National Journal*, 12 July 1986.

19. Under the so-called Beirut Agreement, a 1948 accord among seventy-two nations, documentary film makers can avoid paying import duties and other fees when their work is distributed in foreign countries.

20. Quoted in "U.S. Rules on Documentaries Challenged," *The New York Times*, 6 January 1988.

21. According to a report of the General Accounting Office, between 1980 and 1982, forty-one percent of all foreign films were classified by the Department of Justice as political propaganda.

22. Haig v. Agee, 453 U.S. 280 (1981).

23. For more on this, see *Free Trade in Ideas (A Conference Report)*, published by American Civil Liberties Union, Fund for Free Expression in 1985.

24. Margaret Randall, "Banished from the Land of Her Birth," *The Hartford Courant*, 18 October 1987.

25. "Iran Sales Linked to Wide Program of Covert Policies," *The New York Times*, 15 February 1987. See also "Covert Operations in Central America," *Resource Center Bulletin* (Albuquerque, NM), no. 8 (Winter 1987); and Colleen Roach, "Contragate Scandal and World Media Issues," *Media Monitor* (New Delhi), May/June 1987.

26. A reference to the words of James Madison in 1788: "I believe that there are more instances of the abridgment of the freedom of the people by the gradual and silent encroachments of those in power than by violent and sudden usurpations."

Selected Readings

Brasch, Walter, and Dana Ulloth, eds. *The Press and the State.* Lanham, MD: University Press of America, 1986.

Goldstein, Robert J. *Political Repression in Modern America.* Cambridge, MA: Schenkman, 1978.

Preston, William, and Ellen Ray. "Disinformation and Mass Deception: Democracy as a Cover Story," *Our Right to Know.* New York: Fund for Open Information and Accountability, 1983.

Reporters Committee on Freedom of the Press. *The Reagan Administration and the News Media: A Summary and Analysis of More Than 135 Actions by the Reagan Administration to Restrict the Press.* Washington, DC: Reporters Committee on Freedom of the Press, 1987.

Schorr, Daniel, *Clearing The Air*, Boston: Houghton Mifflin, 1977.

10

A WALL AROUND THE IVORY TOWER

Restrictions on Academic and Scientific Research

In 1986 the Department of Defense ordered that enrollment in a course on metal matrix composites being offered at the University of California at Los Angeles be limited only to U.S. citizens. The reason, the Pentagon said, was that some of the unclassified technical information to be studied was covered by export control regulations.

The UCLA case is one of many examples of the restrictions that have been imposed by the federal government in recent years on the dissemination of scientific and technical information. The Reagan administration in particular was intent on curbing the flow of knowledge abroad. Its policy, based on the belief that lax controls on information in the past had facilitated a Soviet weapons buildup, placed scientists and researchers under a steadily growing body of regulation that was justified by invoking the necessity for national security.

The administration frequently limited attendance at American scientific conferences to U.S. citizens and restricted the circulation of academic papers in a large number of fields. Secrecy has also been spreading on college campuses—where a great deal of federal research is conducted—subjecting growing numbers of academics to the requirement that they submit their writings for prior review by their government sponsors.

Secrecy requirements are eroding the tradition of cooperation among faculty members and researchers, as academics and scientists censor themselves because they fear losing their funding or violating federal regulations. The practices as a whole have created an atmosphere in which government-sponsored research has become yet another area where new rules purportedly aimed at protecting national security are serving to undermine the free exchange of ideas.

The End of the Ivory Tower

For more than a century after the founding of the United States, the academic world remained apart from the pressures of the society at large. Serious threats to academic freedom were few and far between. As late as 1915, a report by the newly formed American Association of University Professors could describe the university as a place where ideas are "stated without fear or favor, which the institution is morally required to respect."[1]

Yet even as the report was released, it seemed clear that the ideal of the autonomous academic oasis was beginning to blur. The coming of World War I brought a wave of domestic political hysteria that reached into academe. Administrators took action against faculty members with unpopular views; those who were considered insufficiently patriotic lost their jobs. At Columbia University, for example, distinguished scholars were dismissed on suspicion of being pro-German, prompting others, including historian Charles Beard, to resign in protest.

This pattern was repeated during the Cold War of the 1940s and 1950s in the form of controls, both official and unofficial, on books, lectures, and the off-campus associations of faculty and students.[2] The House Un-American Activities Committee (HUAC) took considerable interest in teachers who could for any reason be suspected of having Communist affiliations; such accusations, even if groundless, often had serious consequences for a professor's tenure at the university and his or her general standing in the community.

HUAC also targeted college courses. At one point, more than seventy colleges and universities were instructed to submit lists of their textbooks and supplementary readings. Many institutions resisted. The chancellor of Cornell University told committee members that the only way they could find out what texts were being used on his campus was to enroll at the university. The president of the University of Arkansas agreed to send the lists but warned that the university would resist any attempt to interfere with freedom of thought "with every resource at its command."[3]

Generally, however, the anticommunist crusaders, supported by a frightened populace and by presidential administrations that preferred to stay unaware of their most damaging abuses, did succeed in intimidating the academic world. Many institutions succumbed to government censorship and to citizen vigilantism by adopting loyalty tests for faculty members and other forms of self-censorship. The ultraright groups, most of them self-appointed, that hounded liberals as well as leftists met tragically insufficent resistance.

One such powerful organization, the National Council for American Education, financed by "patriotic citizens and companies," listed on its advisory committee nine members of Congress. NCAE carried out a campaign that did not seek to veil its anti-Semitic perspective, hunting between the covers of school texts for anything it might condemn as "un-American." Paul Samuelson's *Economics*, a basic text used in hundreds of college economics courses, was one of the books labeled Marxist in a NCAE publication. The Council's argument: "Now if (1) Marx is Communistic, (2) Keynes is partly Marxian, and (3) Samuelson is Keynesian, what does that make Samuelson and others like him? The answer is clear: Samuelson and the others are mostly part Marxian socialist or Communist in their theories."[4]

The censorship of the McCarthy era was not only ideological; institutions also faced government secrecy regulations that were aimed at preventing Soviet access to atomic and other sensitive research related to the military. The expansion of federally funded scientific research on campus erected barriers to academic freedom that have never been removed.

Targeting the Military-Industrial-University Complex

By the 1960s the anticommunist witch hunts had subsided, but the government's presence at research labs and university campuses continued to expand. With the escalation of the war in Vietnam, many universities became increasingly involved in work for the military. The military-industrial complex that President Eisenhower had warned the country about had now established bases in the academic world.

The complicity of American universities in the military

buildup in Southeast Asia became a major focus of the antiwar movement that emerged on college campuses. Persistent protests—and even some bombings, like the one that demolished the Army Mathematics Research Center at the University of Wisconsin in 1970—forced university administrators to evaluate the extent to which their institutions had been diverted from the pursuit of knowledge to the pursuit of Pentagon grants.[5]

One of the most intense struggles took place in 1969 at the Massachusetts Institute of Technology, one of the academic institutions most deeply tied to the military. Dozens of students and faculty members organized a research stoppage to express concern over the "misuse of scientific and technical knowledge." The groundswell of protest led the MIT administration to agree to explore the possibility of shifting the balance of research in favor of nonmilitary subjects. Nevertheless, government agencies refused to support this reorientation, and it soon became clear that the strategy was not financially feasible. The university decided instead to move the laboratory that received the lion's share of military funds off campus and to sever it administratively from the rest of the university. This legal divestment did little to diminish MIT's involvement in military research.[6]

The antiwar movement challenged but failed to end the presence of the military on campus. By the late 1970s, research connected with national security was once again flourishing in the academic world. Major universities grew increasingly dependent on federal grant money in order to survive. It was thus no surprise that when the federal government began restricting the flow of technical information in the late 1970s, the universities were major targets of the rigid new policies.

Quarantining Information

One of the earliest uses of export controls to limit the dissemination of scientific information had occurred in 1977, when a representative of the National Security Agency warned the Institute of Electrical and Electronics Engineers to suppress some papers scheduled for delivery at a symposium on cryptography.[7]

In the renewed Cold War atmosphere that followed the Soviet invasion of Afghanistan in 1979, federal officials redoubled their attempts to restrict the provision of information and the sale of certain goods to the Soviet bloc. These initiatives were made under the auspices of the Export Administration Act of 1979 (overseen by the Commerce Department) and the Arms Export Control Act of 1968 (enforced by the State Department).

In the midst of major advances in technology, new categories of scientific and technical information were added to the list of items to be restricted. This marked a significant broadening of the earlier objectives of export control (which had been limited to tangible goods of military value), and constituted a major expansion in the government regulation of public information.

The Reagan administration was much more aggressive than previous administrations in controlling technical information, claiming that the lax attitudes of its predecessors resulted in a "massive hemorrhage" of sensitive information to the Soviets. Its view was exemplified in a 1985 letter to fellow cabinet members from Commerce Secretary Malcolm Baldrige, in which he warned of a "give-away program that permits the Soviets to acquire tens of thousands of scientific and technical studies as well as other strategic information."[8]

Baldrige complained specifically about foreign access to data available through his own department's National Technical Information Service—data that, he said, had not been properly classified by other agencies. He tried to set an example to his colleagues by expanding to some 200,000 items the Commerce Department's Critical Control List of material not to be exported to Soviet-bloc countries. The Defense Department followed suit by assembling a 700-page Military Critical Technology List— itself classified—of nonexportable military products and technologies.

Once extended to domestic activities, the scope of federal export regulations began touching on unexpected areas, including libraries and university classrooms. The incident at UCLA was not unique. In repeated instances, foreign students have been barred from certain courses and from using advanced research equipment, including supercomputers.[9] The restrictions on scientists and researchers become particularly dubious once it is understood that a large portion of what the government is trying to protect is readily available on the open market. The acquisition of advanced technology and related information may occur in any number of ways that bear no relation to scientists and researchers, including legal and illegal exports, reexport from legitimate U.S. trading partners, and foreign espionage.[10]

Much of the information and equipment that is restricted under federal regulations inevitably finds its way to anyone willing to pay the price. It was therefore no surprise that by the mid-1980s administration officials were admitting that, despite their efforts, there had been no significant reduction in the unauthorized flow of Western technology to the Soviet Union.[11]

The most powerful argument against export control policies is that technological superiority depends on innovation, which in turn requires open and flexible communication, particularly in the early stages of research. In 1981 the Rand Corporation sponsored a study of how well the Soviets are able to utilize the Western technology they have acquired.[12] The premise of the study was that stringent controls on technology and expertise are necessary only if the Soviet Union is able to utilize what it obtains to some kind of advantage.

Significantly, Thane Gustafson, the principal investigator, found that, except in direct military applications in which the Soviets had considerable expertise and technology of their own, they were unable to introduce acquired technologies; to do so would require changing the basic practices of communication already in place throughout their industrial and research environment. Gustafson concluded that the most effective barriers to the transfer of technology were those erected by the Soviets against themselves. In warning that American restrictions could backfire, he wrote: "History teaches us that control of technology transfer is at best a rear-guard action, achievable (and then only briefly) at the cost of regulations and secrecy that carry harmful side-effects of their own."

Closing Off Communication

A directive signed by President Reagan in 1985 was meant to establish the administration's policy on the dissemination of information derived from basic and applied research. It stated that no restrictions should be placed on "the conduct or reporting of federally-funded fundamental research that has not received national security classification, except as provided in applicable U.S. statutes."[13]

Keep your eye on that final clause. For rather than cut back on restrictions, this directive helps justify a set of censorship rules that goes beyond what Congress has provided in its export-control statutes. The policy does not simply protect classified data. It also applies to information that is in itself "sensitive"—and thus potentially classifiable—as well as to material that could, when combined with other pieces of information, be of some strategic value. This "mosaic" theory reflects the interrelatedness of military and nonmilitary technologies such as computers and satellites, and of corresponding information.

The problem is that this policy potentially encompasses virtually all information in the physical sciences and engineering, and it could even be extended to the social sciences. A paper describing the movement of people from the farms to cities, for example, when combined with information on federal agricultural programs, could be regarded as providing clues to the placement of missile silos. In the name of the unity of knowledge, the federal government could implement this policy to transform all research and analysis into one vast military secret.

This risk can be seen quite clearly in the administration's anxiety about scientific meetings, which it viewed as occasions on which foreign agents can pick up valuable intelligence, thanks to the innocent openness of American researchers.

Government officials have made repeated moves to bar non–U.S. citizens from attending professional-society meetings at which supposedly sensitive topics will be discussed. Groups such as the American Ceramics Society and the American Institute of Aeronautics and Astronautics have given in to government pressure to make proof of citizenship a requirement for admission to certain meetings.

In other cases, government agencies have demanded that certain presentations be canceled entirely. In 1985 the Defense Department ordered the Society of Photo-Optical Instrumentation Engineers to bar the delivery of about a dozen unclassified research papers—for national security reasons. The Energy Department has moved to prevent nuclear engineers from referring to various types of unclassified matters in international meetings.

The federal government's disdain for the tradition of unrestricted, unclassified research has encountered a fair amount of opposition from academic and scientific organizations. A 1982 task force of academic as well as industrial representatives concluded that "security by secrecy" was weakening America's technical capabilities; there was no effective way to restrict international scientific communication, it noted, without also limiting domestic research and development.[14] In 1984 the presidents of Stanford University, the California Institute of Technology, and MIT told the Reagan administration that they would refuse to perform certain kinds of unclassified research for the Pentagon if military reviewers were given the power to restrict the publication of their findings.

Unfortunately, this kind of resistance did little to alter the administration's basic attitude. As in other areas, protest resulted in minor changes without seriously affecting the strong policy of secrecy. Despite the repeated objections to controls on unclassified information, today more material than ever is being restricted, ranging from scientific journals to on-line databases that contain technical information.[15]

Secrecy restrictions weaken the ability of universities to set directions for research. As John Ullman, a computer engineer at Hofstra University, puts it: "Now with Star Wars opening up and conventional funding sources disappearing, there is less and less one can work on that is not classified or restricted in some way or another."

Muzzling the Scientist

Another ominous step away from openness is the policy of requiring large numbers of nongovernment scientists and researchers to sign the same secrecy contracts imposed on government employees (see chapter 7). Standard Form 189A, the version of the contract used for those employed outside government, states:

I have been advised and am aware that direct or indirect unauthorized disclosure, unauthorized retention, or negligent handling of classified information by me could cause irreparable injury to the United States. . . . Any unauthorized disclosure of classified information by me may constitute a violation, or violations, of United States criminal law."[16]

These contracts hold the greatest potential for censorship when they are signed by individuals who are not already subject to security clearances. Especially where future funding depends on agreeing to withhold information, nongovernment employees are likely to engage in self-censorship, caught between choosing the funding of their work or the erosion of their constitutional rights.

The other side of nondisclosure is prior review. Government research contracts increasingly require that researchers submit manuscripts to the National Security Agency, the State Department, or another agency prior to publication. This practice has always been followed in classified research, but now the restrictions are far more sweeping. In the early 1980s, for instance, a number of federally funded researchers found that work that was unclassified at the outset was classified by the government after it was in progress and thus became subject to pre-publication review.

The dangers of this trend have been cited by critics like Robert Park, Director of the American Physical Society, who has observed: "Where there is secrecy, there will be abuses. Prior review limits what gets written as well as what the scientist decides to work on."

Universities are especially vulnerable at a time when federal government funding accounts for some sixty-five percent of money available for research on college campuses. In having become so dependent on federal funds, they have found themselves confronted with a Hobson's choice: Either they assent to government secrecy policies or they lose the grants that are essential to their survival.

The CIA on Campus

The government-induced violations of academic freedom are not limited to the transfer of technology and military research. The 1980s have also seen the return of the Central Intelligence Agency to campuses.

For much of this century the intelligence agencies enjoyed a close relationship with the universities, several of which, especially Yale, were breeding grounds for employees of the elite secret corps.[17] Usually without the knowledge of their colleagues, faculty members in such fields as international relations and anthropology performed research for the intelligence agencies and also agreed to be debriefed by them after foreign field trips. These faculty members also helped recruit intelligence personnel from among their students.

153

The CIA's links to the academic world were revealed in the late 1960s, and activists, alarmed at how university facilities had been compromised, pressured school administrators to banish intelligence work from campuses. The protests were so persistent that many schools adopted policies restricting this kind of research, and CIA campus recruiting was all but abolished. Despite the new climate, some covert CIA-academic programs simply became more discreet. In 1976 the report of the Church Committee on intelligence agency abuses found that the CIA was "now using several hundred academics, who in addition to providing leads and on occasion making introductions for intelligence purposes, occasionally write books and other material to be used for propaganda purposes abroad."[18]

During the Reagan years the CIA restored its overt as well as its covert role on campus. The agency stepped up its campus recruiting efforts, and they continued even after a surge of student protests began in 1985. New efforts were also launched to solidify relationships between the agency and the scholarly world. The CIA began hosting frequent conferences at which its staff analysts were brought together with outside experts. Early in 1986 the agency told *The New York Times* that it was asking academics to review drafts of intelligence estimates prepared by CIA personnel.[19]

During the same period, CIA ties to a particular faculty member caused a controversy at Harvard University, which, in the wake of the Church Committee report, had adopted rules allowing professors to work with intelligence agencies only if the work was done openly. In 1985 it came to light that Nadav Safran, head of Harvard's Center for Middle Eastern Studies, had failed to disclose that the CIA had contributed $45,000 for a conference he had arranged on Islamic fundamentalism. Safran had also received a $107,000 grant from the agency to support research on a book. Following censure by the university, he resigned his post in 1986.

Meanwhile, the CIA pushed ahead with a plan to give it an uncommonly high profile on campus. In 1987 it was revealed that the agency had initiated an officer-in-residence program under which CIA agents were openly installed as visiting scholars on university faculties. A letter from the agency to the political science department at the University of California at Santa Barbara, some of whose members had protested the appointment of CIA veteran George Chritton, Jr., to their faculty, explained that the program was aimed at "providing an opportunity for experienced officers to serve as role models, [and] to counsel interested students on career opportunities with CIA."[20]

University administrators have defended the program in the name of academic freedom, claiming that it exposed students to another point of view. In truth, the granting of academic appointments to CIA officials (who continued to be paid by the agency) provided the intelligence community with an unprecedented legitimate presence in the universities, a presence that can serve only to inhibit the open exchange of ideas.

Corporate-Sponsored Research on Campus

Another challenge to academic freedom is the increased corporate sponsorship of university-based research. Back in the 1950s, business groups tried to impose their influence by pressuring universities to suppress faculty members and texts that criticized the free enterprise system.[21] Today, ideological demands by businesses that fund colleges and universities are less direct, and corporate funders often endorse other kinds of control. Just as military research combines national security considerations with scientific ones, so work performed for business organizations places financial concerns ahead of pedagogical goals. Campus entrepreneurship may please conservative economists, but it does not necessarily make for good education. One study, undertaken for the National Academy of Sciences, found that corporate research puts concern about proprietary information ahead of the tradition of free exchange of ideas.[22]

The possibility of corporate abuse on campus was demonstrated in 1987, when an employee of Fuji Photo Film who had been accepted by the business school at the University of Rochester was later denied admission. The exclusion was prompted by executives of Eastman Kodak, a major university contributor, who feared that the Japanese student might learn inside information about their operations in classes that included many Kodak employees. After the incident was publicized, the university reversed itself, but the student declined the offer, saying: "I didn't know the relationship between the university and Kodak was so strong."[23]

Jonathan Knight, of the American Association of University Professors has described the controls that prevail today on American campuses as "subtle, institutionalized censorship with the greatest potential to corrode scientific freedom." Congress has been concerned enough about the threat that it included in its 1985 amendments to the Export Administration Act the following statement:

> It is the policy of the United States to sustain vigorous scientific enterprise. To do so involves sustaining the ability of scientists and other scholars freely to communicate research findings, in accordance with applicable provisions of law, by means of publication, teaching, conferences, and other forms of scholarly exchange.[24]

To our great loss, this warning has been given little heed by an administration that has devoted itself to restricting the flow of information. Pre-publication review, secrecy contracts, restrictions on attendance at scientific meetings, and other forms of censorship are becoming established practices on the nation's campuses. The main legacy of the Reagan administration in the area of higher education was to change universities from open forums into institutions bedecked with signs reading: "Authorized Personnel Only."[25] It is a climate that we must reverse as soon as possible.

Notes

1. Committee on Academic Freedom and Academic Tenure Report, *AAUP Bulletin* 1 (December 1915).
2. Robert M. MacIver, *Academic Freedom in Our Time: A Study Prepared for the Academic Freedom Project at Columbia University*, (New York: Columbia University Press, 1955).
3. Ibid., p. 115.
4. *Educational Review*, 15 April 1952, described in MacIver, p. 127.
5. Burkholder, Steve, "The Pentagon in the Ivory Tower," *The Progressive*, June 1981. Critiques of campus military research at the time attempted to place it in the wider context of U.S. foreign policy and domestic economic priorities. For example, see Michael Klare, "The Research Apparatus of U.S. Imperialism," *NACLA Newsletter*

1, no.10 (January 1968); and Melman, Seymour, *Pentagon Capitalism* (New York: McGraw-Hill, 1970).

6. Dorothy Nelkin, *The University and Military Research: Moral Politics at M.I.T.* Ithaca, NY: Cornell University Press, 1972.

7. Stephen H. Unger, "The Growing Threat of Government Secrecy," *Technology Review*, February/March 1982, p. 30.

8. Letter of Secretary of Commerce Baldrige, "Soviet Access to Sensitive Scientific and Technical Information Produced by or for the United States Government," 16 January 1985.

9. John Shattuck and Muriel Spence, *Government Information Controls: Implications for Scholarship, Science and Technology* (Cambridge, MA: Harvard University Press, 1988), p. 16.

10. Carol Truxal, "Buying, Selling, and Trading Technology," *IEEE Spectrum*, February 1984, pp. 58–65.

11. "U.S., Despite Technology Curbs, Sees No Big Cut in Flow to Soviet," *The New York Times*, 1 January 1985.

12. Thane Gustafson, *Selling the Russians the Rope? Soviet Technology Policy and U.S. Export Controls* (Rand Corporation, 1981). Much of the information on the Rand study comes from Kathleen Gygi, "Control on Technology Transfer: The Flip Side of Free Flow of Information" (unpublished paper), Interactive Telecommunications Program, New York University, 1985.

13. United States National Security Decision Directive "National Policy on the Transfer of Scientific, Technical and Engineering Information" (NSDD No.189) (Washington, DC: The White House, 21 September 1985).

14. "Scientific Communication and National Security," Report of the Panel on Scientific Communication and National Security, (Washington, DC: National Academy of Sciences, 1982). This report is updated in Mitchell B. Wallerstein, "Scientific Communication and National Security in 1984," *Scientific American* 224 (4 May 1984), pp. 460–466.

15. Charles L. Howe and Robert Rosenberg, "Goverment Plans for Data Security Spill Over to Civilian Networks," *Data Communications*, March 1987.

16. Standard Form 189A, issued November 1985. The information concerning this contract and its application to universities was obtained as part of research financed by the Fund for Investigative Journalism. See Donna Demac, "Sworn to Silence: If You Work For Government Leave the First Amendment Behind," *The Progressive*, May 1987.

17. See Robin W. Winks, *Cloak and Gown: Scholars in the Secret War, 1939–1961* (New York: William Morrow, 1987).

18. Quoted in "'Agents' in Academia are Recruiting Spies," *The New York Times*, 1 January 1978.

19. "C.I.A. Says It Has Restored Link to Campuses to Get More Advice," *The New York Times*, 20 January 1986.

20. Quoted in Jon Wiener, "The CIA Goes Back to College," *The Nation*, 12 December 1987.

21. MacIver, pp. 123–134.

22. "From the Ivory Tower to the Trenches: The University in the High-Tech Race," paper presented by Dorothy Nelkin at Ohio State Conference on Universities and the Future, 8 May 1987. Nelkin was one of the investigators for the NAS study.

23. "University of Rochester Reassessing Kodak Ties After Incident," *Los Angeles Times*, 2 September 1987.

24. Congressional Record 131H:2006 (16 April 1985).

25. An excellent article indicating that controls on unclassified information are likely to increase is Charles L. Howe and Robert Rosenberg, "Government Plans for Data Security Spill Over to Civilian Networks," *Data Communications*, March 1987.

Selected Readings

Dickson, David. *The New Politics of Science*. New York: Pantheon, 1984.

Kaplan, Craig, and Ellen Schrecker, eds. *Regulating The Intellectuals: Perspectives on Academic Freedom in the 1980s*. New York: Praeger, 1983.

Nelkin, Dorothy. *Science as Intellectual Property: Who Controls Scientific Research?* New York: Macmillan, 1984.

Nelkin, Dorothy. *The University and Military Research: Moral Politics at M.I.T.* Ithaca, NY: Cornell University Press, 1972.

Noble, David. *America by Design*. New York: Knopf, 1977.

Salomon, Jean-Jacques. *Science and Politics*. Cambridge, MA: MIT Press, 1973.

Schrecker, Ellen. *No Ivory Tower: McCarthyism in the Universities*. New York: Oxford University Press, 1986.

Shattuck, John, and Muriel Spence. *Government Information Controls: Implications for Scholarship, Science and Technology*. Cambridge, MA: Harvard University Press, 1988.

Tirman, John, ed. The *Militarization of High Technology*. Cambridge, MA: Ballinger, 1984.

Westin, Alan F. *Whistleblowing*. New York: McGraw-Hill, 1981.

11

THE PERSISTENCE OF CENSORSHIP IN THE POST-REAGAN ERA:

The White House and Congress Carry It On

In the fall of 1989, the winds of democracy rose unexpectedly in the East, as millions of people throughout the Soviet bloc demanded greater freedom of expression, association, and travel. In contrast, the United States continued to move in the direction of censorship American style.

One of the trademarks of the new president was his avoidance of controversies that offered little political gain. Bush cultivated the image of the consensus kind of guy, which often made him a latecomer rather than a leader. He waited until the last possible moment before making a statement on the death threat which the late Ayatollah Khomeini issued against author Salman Rushdie and remained silent during the Chinese government's bloody attacks on the prodemocracy students occupying Tiananmen Square.

The Bush team tried hard to present itself as different, and less secretive, than the preceding administration, yet did little to make this convincing. In virtually every area affecting freedom of speech, the restrictive policies of the Reagan era were continued and sometimes intensified.

Bush quickly followed his predecessor's practice of making policy by issuing classified presidential orders and directives, all or part of which were kept secret from Congress as well as the public. The new administration continued the preoccupation with controlling leaks and sought to limit government accountability by classifying large quantities of information.

By the end of 1989, additional curbs on expression were pending in both the executive and legislative branches. Outside government, book banning and "morality" campaigns continued, taking their toll at the local level.

Like a house with termites, policies set in place during the Reagan era virtually guaranteed that open government would continue to decay unless remedial steps were taken both within and outside government.

Securing the Flag

At the end of October 1989, four people shouting "Burn, Baby, Burn," set fire to three American flags on the steps of the Capitol. Their intention was to test the constitutionality of a new federal law banning mutilation of the American flag.

One of the four protesters was Gregory Johnson, who burned the flag at the 1984 Republican Convention in Dallas in order to protest President Reagan's policies on the eve of his renomination. This action set in motion a case that went all the way to the Supreme Court.

In a 1989 decision written by Justice Brennan, the Court ruled 6–3 that Johnson's action was protected speech: "If there is a bedrock principle underlying the First Amendment, it is that the Government may not prohibit the expression of an idea simply because society finds the idea itself offensive or disagreeable."

The Court noted that Johnson was only one of many people who over the years have used the American flag to excite, mock, poke fun, and otherwise provoke great passions. For instance, Abbie Hoffman wore a shirt made out of the American flag at the Chicago Eight trial in 1968.

The Court went on to say that the way to preserve the flag's special role was through persuasion in the marketplace of ideas. "We do not consecrate the flag by punishing its desecration, for in doing so we dilute the freedom that this cherished emblem represents," the Court said.

Due to its resounding confirmation of First Amendment protection even for those who express themselves in less popular ways, the Court's decision was a powerful affirmation of a right Americans are most proud of and which often astonishes people living in countries where dissidents are put in jail. Yet, in this country, the land of the free, the Court's ruling was denounced by the president of the United States.

Bush's response to the Court's decision was to call for a constitutional amendment protecting the flag, claiming that a mere statute would not be strong enough to survive overturning by the Court. Soon politicians from both parties began to fall over one another in their attempts to match the president's revulsion for flag burning.

This seemingly unstoppable force met with little opposition. Surprisingly, even political scientists, lawyers, and others known for their strong support of the First Amendment, supported the call for a law banning rough treatment of the flag; their hope was that this would forestall the move for an amendment. Although their intention was to prevent tampering with the Bill of Rights, the flag legislation itself was a disturbing infringement on free speech.

The Long Shadow of the Iran-Contra Scandal

While the Bush Administration moved ahead with Reagan's policies on secrecy, it was also sweating out an embarrassing consequence of those policies: the trial of Oliver North on charges relating to the Iran-Contra affair. During the 1988 campaign, Bush himself had struggled to escape from the cloud of suspicion surrounding his role in the scandal. Despite his success at the polls, Bush never did answer all the questions concerning his relationship, while vice president, to the illegal funding of the contras.

It was probably in part to protect Bush that the Reagan Administration in its last weeks moved to block North's lawyers from using secret documents that they said were essential for the defense of their client. The release of that classified material, the administration claimed, would be harmful to "national security."

For a while it appeared that Reagan's position, which represented a conflict of interest if there ever was one, would force Judge Gerhard Gesell to conclude that North could not get a fair trial under these conditions and thus the charges against him would have to be dismissed. This use of what some observers called "graymail" did compel Special Prosecutor Lawrence Walsh to withdraw the most serious charges—conspiracy to defraud the United States and theft of government property—against North, though the prosecution continued to press twelve lesser felony counts.

After Bush took office, the conflict over the use of classified material still threatened to delay the trial. The Justice Department made a deal with Walsh under which the Bush administration would have been allowed to review in advance any classified material that would be disclosed in court by North's lawyers. Judge Gesell rejected the plan and later assailed the administration for trying to protect the confidentiality of some documents that were already in the public domain. Gesell said he was facing "an absurd situation in which the press is accurately reporting information in the public domain while the court is confronted with representations that the same facts must never be officially acknowledged."[1]

Despite the Justice Department's maneuvering, the trial of North in the spring of 1989 put Bush in the hot seat once again, at least briefly. One document revealed during the trial suggested that Bush had in 1985 secretly traveled to Honduras to deliver the message to the government of that country that an increase in U.S. military and economic aid was dependent upon continued support for the contras. More evidence also came out about Reagan's personal involvement in the contra aid effort.

North ended up being convicted on three of the twelve charges, but the real significance of the trial was the almost comical way in which information was handled. As Frances FitzGerald has pointed out:

> The North trial was thus on one level a normal courtroom contest, in which the opposing lawyers presented two different versions of events. On another level, it was in itself a modernist drama, for no two groups in the courtroom had the same pool of information at their disposal. The jurors knew only what they heard. The prosecuting attorneys possessed a great deal of secret information they could not reveal or use, but they did not know certain things that the reporters covering the trial knew [because the lawyers had been shielded from congressional testimony covered by immunity]. The defense lawyers, Brendan Sullivan and his team, did not know everything that the prosecution did, but they knew what North knew, and they produced documents that neither the Iran-Contra committees nor the prosecutors had ever seen before.[2]

This information circus was repeated in the cases of other Iran-Contra figures. Attorney General Dick Thornburgh intervened in the prosecution of former CIA official Joseph Fernandez—charged with lying to government investigators about his role in the contra aid effort—to block the use of classified material in the trial. In September 1989 a federal appeals court ruled against Thornburgh, yet he remained adamant in his position. Two months later the judge in the Fernandez case dismissed the charges, saying that a fair trial was not possible without the evidence of the secret documents.

Meanwhile, the judge in the case against North's former boss, John Poindexter, ruled that the defense could subpoena the personal papers and diaries of former President Reagan but not those of the current occupant of the White House. This, however, came after the special prosecutor had announced that he was dropping some of the charges—including conspiracy—against Poindexter to avoid the kind of protracted struggles over government secrets that marked the North case. Overall, it appeared that the stonewalling of the Justice Department, under both Reagan and Bush, paid off in significantly curtailing the prosecution of the Iran-Contra cases.

Befriending the Press, Plugging the Leaks

In his relations with the media George Bush has tried to cultivate an image very different from that of his predecessor. The Reagan administration made no bones about its attempts to "package" the president in the most favorable way and to put its own "spin" on daily television coverage.

Bush, by contrast, has acted as if he is indifferent to the way he is presented in the media. Television correspondents, having grown dependent on eight years of carefully staged photo opportunities and sound bites to use on the evening news, have expressed surprise and even some dismay at Bush's lackadaisical approach. A few months after Bush took office, the *Washington Post* published an article entitled "Press Corps to Bush: Manipulate Us!" The piece quoted CBS correspondent Lesley Stahl as exclaiming: "This White House doesn't care if the president gets on the evening news or not!"[3]

Nonetheless, behind the informal image and the casual meetings with reporters was an administration still preoccupied with controlling the flow of sensitive information to the media. In August 1989 the Justice Department announced that it intended to prosecute officials who leaked information to journalists for theft of government property. Although Attorney General Thornburgh hastened to assure reporters that they would not be prosecuted, the harsh penalties against sources and the warning that journalists could be subpoenaed to testify before grand juries to identify those sources were chilling enough.

A few weeks after the policy was announced, Thornburgh moved to put it into action. The Justice Department threatened to subpoena telephone records of CBS News to try to identify the source of leaks about a criminal investigation of House Majority Whip William Gray. That threat was not carried out, but Thornburgh did pursue the investigation of the leak as a criminal case, sending FBI agents to conduct polygraph examinations of federal employees and impaneling a grand jury.

Thornburgh has also worked to limit the flow of authorized information to the press. He decimated the Justice Department's office of public affairs and warned other officials that they should not talk to reporters, even to give routine information. Thornburgh's effort to make the department speak with one voice—his own—angered the press corps. "It looks a lot like the Bush Campaign," said Charley Roberts, a correspondent for the *Los Angeles Daily Journal*, a law newspaper. "There's a message to get out that day, and nothing else is going to get out."[4]

Bearing Down on the FOIA

As described in earlier chapters, a presidential classification order adopted in 1982 drastically expanded agency authority to classify and reclassify information and thus deny Freedom of Information Act requests. This, in combination with other Reagan administration policies, greatly diminished the act's usefulness, a situation Congress attempted to remedy in amendments to the act passed in 1986.

The legislation overhauled the language pertaining to fee waivers. The 1986 amendments established three categories of users: commercial users (who were required to pay the full expense of search and review time, as well as duplication costs); representatives of the news media and educational and scientific institutions (who only had to pay duplication costs); and all others (who were supposed to pay for the first two hours of search time and the first 100 pages of duplication costs).

The problem was that agencies proceeded to "interpret" the legislation so that a law intended to ease eligibility for fee waivers was instead used as a pretext for sharply reducing access to government records. The Justice Department and Office of Management and Budget issued new FOIA guidelines that, along with other stonewall techniques, gave agencies license to judge the value of the information requested.

In addition, some government agencies began reclassifying users as commercial users. For example, in June 1988, Hardy Green, a writer/historian researching the 1985 strike of the meatpackers union in Austin, Minnesota, submitted an FOIA request to the FBI, seeking documents concerning the Bureau's monitoring of the strike.

The FBI first said that it had found 1,400 documents relevant to the request and that the cost of processing the request would be $130. The writer then waited a full year, only to receive another letter informing him that he had been reclassified as a commercial user (for reasons not specified) and would have to pay $3,500 for the same material.[5]

For news organizations, the reclassification issue was remedied in a 1989 court decision. The Pentagon had refused to recognize the National Security Archive, a nonprofit research group that works with the press on a wide range of issues, as a media organization. However, the court ruling on this declared that the 1986 amendments were intended to facilitate access by the press and included any entity that "gathers information of potential interest to a segment of the public, uses its editorial skills to turn the raw materials into distinct work, and distributes that work to an audience."[6] This reading included not only the archive but a wide range of other media and research organizations.

Another serious obstacle to obtaining government documents was the refusal of many agencies (federal and state) to extend their obligations under the Freedom of Information Act to the enormous volume of information stored electronically. People requesting this information were hit with denials on the grounds that information in data bases did not constitute "records" within the meaning of the act; or that the process of retrieving such information required the agency to create a new record—not something agencies must do under the act; or that the need to conduct an electronic search would substantially increase the amount the user was required to pay.

Those concerned about ensuring that the FOIA is applied to electronic information disagree as to whether new legislation is needed to broaden its scope.[7] Those who oppose such action argue that the act is already explicit about the goal of providing the fullest possible disclosure and that court decisions are the best way to bring about agency reform, without risking unwanted changes in the law.

So far courts have generally, though not always, ruled that electronic records are no different from paper records. Yet no one knows just how many court decisions will be necessary. Until the magic number has been reached, or until new FOIA legislation is passed, cramped readings of the law make it more likely than ever that initial FOIA requests will be denied and individual requesters will be faced with the costly challenge of taking the agency to court.

The Perils of a Government Job

Several of the curbs on civil liberties that were being tightened in the late 1980s affected the millions of people who work for the federal government, either as agency personnel or as employees of firms for whom the government is a primary client. These people feel the government's power most directly and have been required to abide an expanding list of intrusive regulations, including polygraph examinations, drug testing, and lifetime secrecy agreements.

Of all the secrecy edicts announced while Ronald Reagan was in office, perhaps none evoked as much opposition as the 1983 presidential directive which, among other things, obligated current and former government employees to sign lifetime secrecy contracts forbidding disclosure of classified and "classifiable" information. Various critics argued that just the fear associated with signing such a contract would serve as a gag order, severely limiting public access to vital information and inhibiting the oversight function of Congress.

The opposition to this action was so intense that Reagan, in a second announcement, said he would not enforce key provisions of the directive. This was generally thought to have put the matter to rest but, in reality, it merely deflected public criticism while agencies proceeded to implement the directive. By late 1989 secrecy contracts had been signed by approximately three and a half million people, according to the head of the Information Security Oversight Office, which oversees executive branch security programs.[8]

Successive efforts by Congress to halt this practice through legislation prohibiting the term "classifiable" and limiting the scope of the agreement proved unsuccessful. Though the government agreed to eliminate the word "classifiable,"[9] federal agencies otherwise defied the legislation.[10]

In late 1989, Congress continued negotiations over use of the secrecy contracts and passed for a third time language aimed at limiting their enforcement.[11] But the White House lost no time in putting out a "Statement by the President" that instructed agencies to ignore the legislation.

Are You Now or Have You Ever . . . ?

Those who complain of the burdens imposed by government paperwork never include the onerous threats to individual privacy posed by forms that people applying for or holding government positions must complete.

Beginning in 1989, an amended employee questionnaire was introduced which resurrected questions about communist and other political affiliations (Question 30a: "Have you ever been a member, officer, or employee of the Communist Party?"). These questions had been eliminated in the 1970s due to court decisions which suggested that such questions might be unconstitutional.

The form also demanded answers to questions about individuals' medical histories (Question 25: "Have you ever had a nervous breakdown or have you ever had medical treatment for a mental condition?"), alcohol and drug use (Question 24b: "Do you now use or supply, or within the last five years have you used or supplied, marijuana, cocaine, narcotics, hallucinogens, or other dangerous or illegal drugs?"), and organizational affiliations.

According to Frank Askin, a law professor at Rutgers University, the form indicated that "a new ideological witchhunt involving federal employees and applicants for employment" had begun. Particularly significant, according to Askin, was that the form was being used to evaluate not only employees with access to secret information but also a sprawling new category: those in "sensitive" jobs.[12]

As the new form was introduced, large numbers of people were reclassified into the "sensitive" category. At the Bureau of Indian Affairs, for example, all employees who came into contact with children, such as schoolteachers, were put in this category.

Gary Stern of the ACLU Washington office said part of the motivation appeared to be "the bureaucratic desire for one form that could be used for all employees." However, the bureaucracy's interest in an omnibus form could hardly justify this new attempt to bind employees to regulations that made the surrender of privacy rights the price for keeping one's job.

Targeting the Right of Due Process

Shortly after President Bush took office, a draft of a presidential order on security clearances was circulated, which would grant agency heads sweeping authority to deny security clearances to federal workers and employees of government contractors without giving them the reason for the denial or the chance to respond.

This meant that millions of people, whose jobs required security clearances every five years, would be at risk of losing their jobs, without ever knowing why. For people old enough to remember the 1950s, when many people lost their jobs and homes solely on the basis of rumors they were powerless to correct, this order had an ominous ring.

Though the government's power to hire and fire is not often challenged successfully,[13] in theory most federal employees are entitled to a written explanation as to why their security clearance had been denied—to the fullest extent consistent with national security—and an opportunity to rebut the accusations and appeal the decision. The proposed order would completely eliminate this basic right of due process and take the government-citizen relationship one step closer to what one commentator has called "the new feudalism."[14]

168

Recycling an old rationale, Bush Administration officials said that the proposed order was the outcome of work begun under Reagan to stop unauthorized disclosures of secret information.[15] In fact, this order was a vivid illustration of how a presidential order parading under the banner of national security can easily become a tool for depriving individuals of their constitutional rights, including due process and freedom of expression.

Surveillance: Spies in the Library

Ray Bradbury had it right. In his futuristic novel *Fahrenheit 451*, libraries are the enemies of the totalitarian world he presents. Underground fugitives have memorized books to pass on to later generations; collectively, they are the only remaining library.

In the 1980s, librarians have surely found themselves on the front lines. In addition to the struggles described in earlier chapters concerning book banning, the privatization of government information and pressures to restrict access to certain categories of unclassified material, librarians across the country at academic, specialized, and public libraries have been pressed to disclose the names and reading habits of certain library patrons to the FBI.

The "Library Awareness Program" first came to public attention in September 1988. Just months earlier, Paula Kaufman, a librarian at Columbia University who had been visited by two FBI agents, contacted the American Library Association Office of Intellectual Freedom in Chicago. She wrote: "[The FBI] explained that they were doing a general library awareness program in the city and that they were asking librarians to be alert to the use of their libraries by persons hostile to the U.S. such as the Soviet Union, and to provide information about these activities." No guidelines were given to determine which library users might be hostile to the United States. "In a multicultural, multiethnic society, how do you determine someone who is a foreigner?" she asked.

In its response to public and congressional objections, the FBI showed more than ever that the mentality of the Hoover era was still operative. It first maintained that the program was being carried out only at specialized scientific and technical libraries in New York City. This was soon refuted by several independent studies which showed the program was being conducted in cities throughout the country.[16]

The American Library Association received descriptions of twenty-five visits to libraries from New York City to Los Angeles.[17] In one case where agents were dissatisfied with the outcome of a library visit, they used telephone taps and hidden cameras on reference desks, and followed up with a visit to a library staff member's home.[18]

Several FOIA requests, as well as congressional hearings and a lawsuit, were required to pry information about the program out of the Bureau. Eventually some two thousand pages of documentary evidence were released.

Meantime, the game of "catch us if you can" continued. At a Senate Judiciary Committee hearing in May 1988 FBI Director William Sessions defended the library program as a counter-espionage operation against the Soviet effort to gain sensitive technical information and recruit agents.

The same month the FBI released a thirty-three-page report, "The KGB and the Library Target," prepared by the Intelligence Division at FBI headquarters. It described a "massive" Soviet effort, spanning several decades, to penetrate America's specialized scientific and technical libraries, including such dangerous activities as the use of data bases and reference works; the development of librarians as sources of information; and the reproduction of microfiche.

A month later, Representative Don Edwards, himself a former FBI agent, and chair of the Judiciary Subcommittee on Civil and Constitutional Rights, held hearings on the program. Library representatives testified that what the Bureau was asking for was illegal in thirty-six states that had "Confidentiality of Library Records" statutes.

Sessions later attempted to silence the criticism by telling Edwards that he had issued new guidelines which confined the program to public, university, and corporate libraries in the New York City area and that the cooperation of librarians would be voluntary. But there were soon indications that this was only Bureau doublespeak. A FBI spokesman told reporters that this was not a cutback but was only intended to "dispel the myths about the program."

Not only did the Library Awareness Program continue, but

it came out that the Bureau was investigating librarians and other individuals who had publicly criticized the program.

The Nine Lives of Government Surveillance

Regarding surveillance of dissident groups, as with its relations with the press, the Bush Administration has tried to project a more benevolent image. The FBI continued its policy of admitting that the Reagan Administration's program of surveillance and harassment of opponents of its Central America policy had gotten out of hand. In the final months of Reagan's term of office, the Bureau admitted mistakes had been made, and several middle and low-level officials were suspended or disciplined for what was described as excessive zeal in pursuing the investigation of the Committee in Solidarity with the People of El Salvador (CISPES) and other groups.

Not satisfied with this scapegoating of a few inconsequential Bureau employees who were in all likelihood following orders from higher up, the victims of the FBI abuses brought suit against the Bureau. As a result of this action, the FBI agreed in November 1989 to purge its files of thousands of names of people and organizations collected during the investigation.

At about the same time, the Bureau also acknowledged that it had been engaged in an effort to investigate and disrupt the National Lawyers Guild, almost from the moment the progressive organization was formed in 1937. Settling an eleven-year-old lawsuit, the FBI agreed to transfer the data collected on the guild to the National Archives, where it will be sealed until the year 2025.[19]

Yet the willingness to make a few mea culpas for the excesses of the Reagan years and the Hoover era should not lead one to assume that the FBI has totally cleaned up its act. According to David Cole of the Center for Constitutional Rights, which represented the victims of the FBI CISPES abuses, the Bureau has continued its repressive policies "with at least as much if not more vigor under Bush than during the Reagan Administration."

One indication of this has come in the case of the L.A. Eight, a group of seven Palestinians and a Kenyan whom the government has sought to deport because of their involvement in an organization advocating Palestinian rights. The FBI and the Immigration and Naturalization Service have admitted that they engaged in surveillance of the attorneys representing the members of the L.A. Eight, including wiretapping of lawyer-client conversations. The lawyers include ones working with the American Civil Liberties Union and the Center for Constitutional Rights.

Kate Martin of the ACLU says that although surveillance of the lawyers began in 1987, there is no evidence that the practice ended with the installation of the Bush administration. Attorney General Thornburgh, who took office after the resignation of Ed Meese in 1988 and who is a defendant in a suit brought by the subjects of the surveillance, was asked by President Bush to remain in that position.

The Bush administration's unwillingness to break from the covert practices of the past is even clearer when it comes to foreign operations. The CIA, once headed by the man who is now in the White House, has pushed for greater latitude in conducting the kind of foreign escapades that led to fiascos in the past. The main difference, according to Gary Stern of the ACLU Washington Office, is that Bush "seems to want approval in advance in order to avoid the need to lie to Congress presented in the Iran-Contra situation."

Not every situation provided opportunities for such cooperation. At one point, the CIA attempted to defeat a Senate proposal to create an inspector general appointed by the president to investigate wrongdoing in the agency. Then, in October 1989, CIA Director William Webster called on Congress to give the agency greater freedom to support foreign coups that could lead to the killing of a country's leader. Webster's request amounted to a call for rescinding an executive order adopted in 1976 by President Ford. The order, which followed revelations about CIA involvement in plots to kill Fidel Castro and other foreign leaders, barred U.S. involvement in such assassination efforts.

Webster suggested that the restriction had undermined U.S. assistance to Panamanian forces that unsuccessfully tried to oust the Noriega government several weeks earlier. Although Congress showed some willingness to go along with a greater freedom to kill, the administration decided to go back and reinterpret the 1976 executive order in a way that led to the same conclusion. The Justice Department lawyers decided that the order did allow the United States to support violent coups, as long as murdering the country's leader was not an explicit goal. In other words, the CIA was free to go around overthrowing governments as long as they had the solemn word of their local cronies that the ousted leader would not be executed. This is what passes for "reform" of covert operations in the Bush era.

Helms and the NEA

The urge to censor continues to be seen in Congress as well as in the executive branch. This impulse reached new heights in the summer of 1989 with the uproar over the fact that federal money had supported, in part, an art exhibit that included pieces denounced by North Carolina Senator Jesse Helms as "immoral trash."[20] The new climate of intolerance had been ushered in a few months earlier by the reaction to a work, which was part of an exhibit in The Art Institute of Chicago, that displayed an American flag on the floor and invited viewers to "confront their feelings" about symbols and step on the flag if they so chose.

The next outrage, according to the guardians of decency, was an exhibit mounted by the Institute of Contemporary Art in Philadelphia. The show was a retrospective of photographer Robert Mapplethorpe, who died of AIDS in March 1989 and whose work included a strong homoerotic element. The exhibit, which had received $30,000 from the National Endowment for the Arts, was supposed to open 1 July at the Corcoran Gallery in Washington. It was cancelled shortly before the opening out of concern by Corcoran officials that Mapplethorpe's sexually explicit photographs would have political repercussions on Capitol Hill.

The Corcoran cancellation served only to fuel the controversy, although the show found another exhibition space in Washington. Congress did indeed express its displeasure with the Mapplethorpe photographs, and with another NEA-funded exhibit in Winston-Salem, North Carolina, that included a photograph by Andres Serrano depicting a plastic crucifix submerged in the artist's urine.

In July the House voted to cut the $45,000 that had been granted to the two exhibits from the NEA's budget, while the

Senate approved a measure proposed by Helms to bar the two institutions involved in the controversial exhibits from receiving NEA grants for five years. Just before its August recess a nearly deserted Senate also approved a Helms measure to ban the use of federal funds for art that is "obscene or indecent," that "denigrates the objects or beliefs of . . . a particular religion or non-religion," or that "denigrates, debases or reviles . . . on the basis of race, creed, sex, handicap, age, or national origin."

The sweeping Helms measure outraged the artistic community, which organized protests in cities across the country. At a Los Angeles demonstration, works by artists like Van Gogh and Picasso who had been censored at one time were projected onto a wall of the federal building. A statement from actress Whoopi Goldberg said, "Without freedom of artistic expression, we have no culture. Without a culture we have no identity as a nation. Rather [we are] the United States of sheep."[21]

Congress acted slightly less herdlike when a House-Senate conference committee rejected the Helms measure. Nevertheless, the committee approved legislation which prevented the NEA from funding art that was legally obscene and established a commission to review the endowment's grant procedures.

The NEA got the message. Shortly after the new law was signed by President Bush, the endowment withdrew its sponsorship of a New York exhibit on AIDS whose catalogue criticized public figures, including Senator Helms. In a letter to the executive director of the gallery, Artists Space, which mounted the show, NEA chairman John Frohnmayer said, "We must all work together to insure that projects funded by the Endowment do not violate either the spirit or the letter of the law."[22]

Facing another uproar from the artistic world, including a reported decision by composer Leonard Bernstein to refuse the National Medal of the Arts, Frohnmayer later restored the $10,000 grant to the gallery and promised to work for the removal of the law restricting endowment grants to art considered obscene. Yet there was a catch: The $10,000 could not be used to pay for the show's controversial catalogue, which Frohnmayer insisted was political rather than artistic in nature and thus not a proper use of NEA funds. Ironically, Artists Space ended up paying for the catalogue with a grant from the Robert Mapplethorpe Foundation.

Although the main parties involved seemed to be satisfied

with this compromise, the Frohnmayer position on "political" material is even more chilling than the crusade against "obscene" art. As Richard Goldstein put it in the *Village Voice*, "To subject an artist's work to a litmus test of political probity—and punish institutions that will not carry out the mandate of the state—is to traffic in the thought control that gave us Stalinism and Nazism (not to mention McCarthyism)."[23]

The Anti-Porn Fetish Heats Up

Although Attorney General Edwin Meese left office in July 1988 under a cloud of suspicion regarding his business dealings, the impact of his pornography commission continued to be felt during the final months of the Reagan Administration and into the Bush era.

The Justice Department continued with its policy of using the racketeering (RICO) law to try to put purveyors of supposedly obscene material out of business. For a while the future of this tactic was in question as the feds awaited a Supreme Court ruling on a challenge made to an Indiana racketeering statute. In its February 1989 ruling the high court gave a mixed message. The justices ruled unanimously that the First Amendment barred law enforcement officials from seizing the inventory of "adult" bookstores before a court had determined that the material was obscene. The ability to seize assets used in an alleged racketeering enterpise before trial is one of the most powerful aspects of the RICO law.

However, the Court did not agree with the argument of the bookstore owners that the First Amendment barred the use of the RICO law altogether in obscenity cases. Justice White, speaking for the majority in the 6–3 decision on this point, acknowledged that the harsh penalties in the RICO statute might lead some booksellers to "practice self-censorship and remove material protected by the First Amendment from their shelves," but he insisted that "the deterrence of the sale of obscene materials is a legitimate objective of state anti-obscenity laws."

The Justice Department has also continued making use of the Meese Commission's practice of intimidation. In August 1989 a letter on FBI stationery arrived at the offices of Priority Records in Los Angeles. Milt Ahlerich, assistant director of the

Bureau's office of public affairs, expressed concern about a song recorded by the rap group N.W.A. called "_ _ _ _ Tha Police" (the group sings "fuck the police" but the album cover uses the blanks). Claiming that the album, distributed by Priority, "encourages violence against and disrespect for the law enforcement officer," Ahlerich said ominously, "I wanted you to be aware of the FBI's position relative to this song and its message. I believe my views reflect the opinion of the entire law enforcement community."[24]

That last phrase is significant. The FBI was apparently "tipped off" about N.W.A. by police officials in several cities who, in turn, started getting warnings about the group after an article appeared in a right-wing Christian publication called *Focus on the Family Citizen*, published by Reverend James C. Dobson. That article, which urged readers to "alert local police to the dangers they may face in the wake of this record release," was written by Bob DeMoss, who had previously worked with Tipper Gore's Parents' Music Resource Center.[25] This confluence of the Christian Right, the FBI, and PMRC, with its well-connected founders (including Susan Baker, the wife of the secretary of state), constitutes a frightening force for censorship.

The spirit of Meese also lingers in Congress. In 1988 numerous representatives and senators got on a bandwagon aimed at passing more restrictive child pornography laws. Although strong laws already existed in this area (and had been upheld by the Supreme Court), the legislators decided that federal prosecutors needed better tools to go after child porn merchants.

However, when Congress passed the Child Protection and Obscenity Enforcement Act it went overboard. The most controversial part of the law was the attempt to thwart the use of children in the production of potentially obscene material by requiring producers of sexually explicit books, magazines, films, and videotapes to keep careful records of the ages of the actors and models employed. The record-keeping requirements also applied to those involved in the distribution of the works.

In 1989 a coalition of groups involved in publishing and entertainment filed a suit challenging the constitutionality of the law, arguing that it effectively prevented legitimate publishers and producers from distributing material with any sexual content. A federal court agreed. In May 1989 U.S. District Judge George Revercomb struck down the parts of the law dealing with record-keeping, saying that they "infringe too deeply on the right to produce First Amendment–protected material."[26] Yet Revercomb left intact other provisions of the law, including those sanctioning the use of the RICO law against pornographers.

Congress also attempted to pull the plug on the burgeoning "dial-a-porn" business. Yet the legislation passed in 1988 extended the ban to "indecent" as well as obscene telephone services, which put the law in direct conflict with established First Amendment protections. Consequently, in June 1989 the Supreme Court unanimously struck down the part of the law dealing with telephone messages that were not legally obscene. Justice White wrote that the law, prompted by concerns that children might be exposed to the sexually explicit messages, had "the invalid effect of limiting the content of adult telephone conversations to that which is suitable for children to hear. It is another case of burning up the house to roast the pig."

Sanitizing the Airwaves

Congress and the Federal Communications Commission engaged in more "house burning" relating to the regulation of controversial radio and television broadcasts. The FCC moved ahead with its 1987 policy on "indecent" programming by fining a Kansas City, Missouri, TV station for airing during prime time a film called *Private Lessons* which included some scenes of a woman's bare breasts and buttocks.[27]

The FCC was forced to limit its indecency ban as a result of a 1988 decision by the U.S. Court of Appeals. The court ruled that the FCC had not adequately justified extending the ban on "indecent" programming, which originally covered midnight to 6 A.M, back to 10 P.M. But the three-judge panel did uphold extending the morning ban to 10 A.M.

Congress came to the rescue of the FCC's bluenoses by passing legislation, introduced by Senator Helms, that allowed the commission to apply its indecency rules to programming at any time of the day or night. Although the twenty-four-hour ban was postponed by a federal appeals court, the commission continued its crusade. Emboldened by the law and by the encouragement of several senators during his confirmation hearing, Alfred Sikes, the FCC chairman appointed by President Bush, initiated indecency actions against three radio stations only seventeen days after taking office. The three stations, in Chicago, Indianapolis, and San Jose, California, were cited for off-color language used by so-called shock jock announcers. Then in October 1989 the commission fined four other radio stations for violating the indecency rules and notified several others that they were being investigated. One of the fined stations, WIOD-AM of Miami, was penalized $10,000 for playing song parodies such as "Penis Envy" and Walk with an Erection."

The Aftermath of Hazelwood

Censorship has also continued to spread in the nation's educational institutions. In the wake of the Supreme Court's 1988 ruling in the Hazelwood case, high school principals across the country have been making good use of their new right to regulate the content of student publications. The Student Press Law Center reported in January 1989 that it had received hundreds of complaints about censorship in the twelve months since the high court handed down its decision.

"We are hearing increasing reports of school principals and superintendents actually banning certain stories or entire topics from student newspapers and yearbooks," said Mark Goodman, the center's executive director. "Typically, the censored articles involve criticism of school officials or policies or discussion of important social issues like drug abuse or AIDS."[28]

Sometimes the reasons for the censorship were more mundane. In one Michigan high school the superintendent barred publication of a letter to the editor critical of a local tanning salon that was also one of the paper's major advertisers.[29]

Advocates of student press freedom took some solace in the discovery that state laws and regulations often provided some of the protections the Hazelwood decision had taken away. The model was a 1983 California statute that limited the right of school officials to regulate content to cases where the material is "obscene, scandalous, or slanderous" or "which so incites students as to create a clear and present danger of the commission of unlawful acts on school premises or the violation of lawful school regulations, or the substantial disruption of the orderly operation of the school." Post-Hazelwood legislation protecting student rights has been enacted in Massachusetts and Iowa.

There have also been more direct attacks on the Hazelwood ruling. At Ridgefield High School in Connecticut, students and advisers involved in producing a literary magazine called *Lodestar* filed suit in federal court against the school's ban on material written by alumni. In March 1989 a U.S. District Court issued a preliminary injunction prohibiting the school from enforcing its policy. The court said that the Hazelwood decision did not apply to all student publications; those that operate as an independent student activity, rather than simply a school activity, may be beyond the reach of the Supreme Court decision.

Another challenge to Hazelwood came in the case of a student at Northport High School in New York who had written a story for a student literary magazine. The superintendent of the school barred distribution of the magazine because the story, written by Eric Brenner, contained what the superintendent deemed "inappropriate" language, including the words "dick" and "pee." The National Coalition Against Censorship helped Brenner appeal the action to the New York State education commissioner. The commissioner overruled the superintendent, saying that the school district had not followed its own rules and that state policies provided broad protection of student expression.

The Indefatigable Book Banners and Creationists

The Hazelwood decision has also been exploited by the book banners. Shortly after the high court ruling, a federal district court in Florida used the decision to uphold a county school board's banning of a state-approved humanities textbook. The book was censored because it included Chaucer's "Miller's Tale" from *Canterbury Tales* and *Lysistrata* by Aristophanes. The attack on the books began with a letter from a local minister denouncing the Aristophanes play as "pornography and women's lib" and the Chaucer story as "crass humor" that was "inappropriate reading for anyone."[30] In 1989 the U.S. Court of Appeals upheld that ruling, again citing the Hazelwood precedent.

The self-appointed moral guardians don't limit their interference to high schools; they also go after college courses. On New York's Long Island a group with the misleading name Citizens for a More Informed America protested a course at Nassau Community College called Family Life and Human Sexuality. The group denounced the course as "pornographic" and "morally ambiguous." The citizens group complicated the case by demanding to see a film and other materials used in the course, arguing that because the school was a public institution, the state freedom of information act allowed them such access. As of this writing, a state court is trying to sort out the competing claims of academic freedom and public access to information.

The forces of fundamentalism have also continued their crusade to undermine the teaching of evolution in the schools. After the California Board of Education in early 1989 announced a firm policy on including evolution and excluding creationism from science textbooks, the Christian Right launched a counterattack. The creationists lobbied intensively for "equal time" in the curriculum. They failed in that objective, but the board's guidelines for textbook publishers deleted the statement that "there is no scientific dispute that evolution has occurred and continues to occur" and replaced it with the more hesitant description of evolution as "both a fact and a theory."[31]

Notes

1. David Johnston, "Judge in North Case Assails U.S. Over Handling of Secret Material," *New York Times*, 8 March 1989.

2. Frances FitzGerald, "Annals of Justice: Iran-Contra," *New Yorker*, 16 October 1989, p. 54.

3. David Ignatius, "Press Corps to Bush: Manipulate Us!" *Washington Post*, 7 May 1989, p. B1.

4. Quoted in Kenneth Jost, "General Thornburgh Cuts Off the Press," *Washington Journalism Review*, November 1989, p. 41.

5. Telephone conversation with Hardy Green, 24 November 1989.

6. National Security Archive v. Department of Defense, U.S. Court of Appeals (D.C. Circuit, 7/28/89).

7. Jerry Berman, "The Right to Know: Public Access to Electronic Information," in *New Directions in Telecommunications Policy*, ed. Paula R. Newburg (Durham, N.C.: Duke University Press, 1989).

8. This was the figure cited by Steven Garfinkel, head of the Information Security Oversight Office, which oversees

implementation of the form, in a telephone conversation with the author on 20 November 1989.

9. The change in terminology required the use of a new form, which, though it did not use the word "classifiable," authorized termination of one's job and prosecution for disclosing information "that meets the standards for classification and is in the process of a classification determination."

10. Agencies' refusal to follow the legislation prompted a lawsuit filed by the Public Citizen Litigation Group on behalf of the American Foreign Service Association and seven members of Congress. It went before a judge who ruled that Congress, in passing the law, had interfered with the president's "sovereign prerogative" over national security information. Subsequently, the case was appealed to the Supreme Court which sent it back to the first court with instructions to determine the effect of developments after the lawsuit was filed, including deletion of the word classifiable. Because of the importance of the constitutional issues involved, it emphasized that the "District Court should not pronounce on the relative constitutional authority of Congress and the Executive Branch unless it finds it imperative to do so."

11. This language was section 618 of the Treasury, Postal Service and General Government Appropriations Act for Fiscal Year 1990 (H.R.2989).

12. Frank Askin, telephone interview with the author, 9 November 1989.

13. In 1988, the Supreme Court ruled 6–3 that a civilian navy employee did not have a right to appeal denial of a security clearance. Department of the Navy v. Egan, 484 U.S. 518 (1988).

14. Charles Reich, "The New Property," *Yale Law Journal* 73, p. 733

15. Statements made suggested that the proposed order on security clearances dated back to the presidential directive signed by Reagan in 1983 which required government employees to sign lifetime secrecy contracts and significantly expanded polygraph testing for government employees suspected of disclosing information.

16. Researchers found that, beginning in the 1960s, FBI agents had visited libraries as part of a counterintelligence "awareness" program, at times referred to in bureau documents as the Development of Counterintelligence Awareness Among Librarians, or DECAL. The objective was to warn about possible KGB recruitment or research activities.

17. Natalie Robins, "Spying in the Stacks: The F.B.I.'s Invasion of Libraries," *Nation*, 9 April 1988, pp. 498–502. In a subsequent article, "Library Follow Up," *Nation*, 25 June 1988, p. 885, Robins said she had located fourteen libraries in ten states that had been visited by the FBI over the past six years.

18. Nancy Kranich, "The KGB, The FBI and Libraries," *Our Right*

to Know, Summer 1988. Kranich is director of Public and Administrative Services of New York University Libraries.

19. It was revealed in August 1988 that from 1932 to at least 1985 the Bureau had conducted surveillance, including wiretaps, of several members of the Supreme Court: See "FBI Kept File on Supreme Court," *New York Times*, 21 August 1988.

20. Quoted in Glenn Collins, "On Helms and Grants with Poison Pills," *New York Times*, 7 August 1989.

21. Quoted in Amei Wallach, "The Funding Fight," *New York Newsday*, 5 September 1989, section II, p. 8.

22. Quoted in William H. Honan, "Arts Endowment Withdraws Grant for AIDS Show," *New York Times*, 9 November 1989, p. 1.

23. Richard Goldstein, "Editorial: Mr. Frohnmayer's Wall," *Village Voice*, 21 November 1989, p. 3.

24. The text of the letter was reproduced in Dave Marsh and Phyllis Pollack, "Wanted for Attitude," *Village Voice*, 10 October 1989, p. 33. Additional information appears in Richard Harrington, "On the Beat: The FBI as Music Critic; Letter on Rap Record Seen as Intimidation," *Washington Post*, 4 October 1989, p. B7.

25. These details come from Marsh and Pollack, "Wanted for Attitude."

26. Quoted in Tracy Thompson, "Parts of Child Pornography Law Struck Down," *Washington Post*, 17 May 1989, p. A19.

27. In 1989 the FCC rescinded the fine for technical reasons relating to the Court of Appeals decision.

28. Student Press Law Center, "Student Newspaper Censorship on the Rise," press release, 4 January 1989.

29. "School Officials Yank Letter to Editor," *Student Press Law Center Report*, Fall 1988, p. 21.

30. Quoted in *Censorship News* (National Coalition Against Censorship), Issue 26, 1987, p. 1.

31. Seth Mydans, "Correction: California Terms Evolution 'Fact,'" *New York Times*, 14 November 1989.

Selected Readings

Curry, Richard O., ed. *Freedom At Risk: Secrecy, Censorship, and Repression in the 1980s*. Philadelphia: Temple University Press, 1988.

Hertsgaard, Mark. *On Bended Knee: The Press and the Reagan Presidency*. New York: Farrar Straus Giroux, 1988.

Marx, Gary T. *Undercover: Police Surveillance in America*. Berkeley and Los Angeles: University of California Press, 1988.

Schultz, Bud, and Ruth Schultz. *It Did Happen Here: Recollections of Political Repression in America*. Berkeley and Los Angeles: University of California Press, 1989.

12

A TIME TO SPEAK OUT

The Future of Free Expression in America

As this book shows, censorship takes many forms in America today. It may come about through the issuance of a presidential order, the pursuit of "paperwork reduction," the dismissal of a corporate whistleblower, the filing of a libel suit, or the crusade of self-appointed guardians of decency. The culprits, whether government officials or private groups, employ a variety of techniques, some of them borrowed from earlier periods of repression, others new. Whatever their form, these attempts to control free expression and deny access to information have placed the cherished rights of the citizens of this country in jeopardy.

In too many areas, significant threats to freedom of expression have been ignored, swept under the carpet, or excused by pointing to worse alternatives or greater infringements elsewhere. While it is undoubtedly true that the American system of government protects freedom of speech more than do the governments of other countries, rationalizations based on such comparisons are neither patriotic nor even relevant. Instead, they serve only to justify avoiding the task of addressing the subtle and incremental institutional restrictions on expression that are becoming entrenched in our society.

Rationalizations might even be considered subversive. After all, the right of free speech is at the center of American liberty, and the exercise of that right is basic to American democracy.

Justifications and exemptions for curbs on expression undermine our entire framework of constitutional government.

The ban on press coverage during the Grenada invasion, the FCC's crackdown on "indecency" on radio and television, the federal government's curtailment and abandonment of vital information programs, the distortion of statistics on severe social problems like hunger and homelessness, the expansion of private surveillance groups that infiltrate legitimate political organizations, the brushfire of book banning campaigns, and many other assaults on individual liberty could not have gone ahead if many Americans had not underestimated their importance.

During the Reagan era the combined forces of government and private organizations sought to roll back the openness and the greater political participation that were achieved in the struggles of the recent past. Right-wing religious and social organizations were encouraged in the campaigns they waged against feminist, gay, environmental, antinuclear, and even educational associations. While campaigning for one's own values is the essence of American democracy, these attacks have often involved deliberate efforts to prevent certain groups from exercising their constitutional rights. What has been particularly chilling about them is that many of their victims have had to face their accusers with little organized support from the rest of the country.

Why has there not been more uproar about these efforts at eroding the social gains of the entire post–World War II era? Drawing public attention to political issues and values that were actively opposed by the Reagan agenda has been extremely difficult. The administration's great skills at public relations to a great degree succeeded in shutting out from mainstream discourse those who did not support its policies. But if we tolerate these restrictions in silence, we spite ourselves and our country.

As a result of censorship, local institutions and neighborly relations that promote tolerance and pride of place have been weakened. Fundamentalist parents confidently challenge school-teachers who put up Halloween decorations in their classrooms. The desire to escape the fear of religious persecution is what brought the original settlers to this continent, and it is disturbing to see persecution by religious radicals undermining individual freedom in our time. One of the purposes of this report is to situate the current threats to the freedom of expression in their historical context, for awareness of earlier First Amendment battles enhances any understanding about the necessity to correct present-day limitations on expression.

Supply-Side Secrecy

The Reagan government demonstrated more clearly than any previous administration the power of the executive branch to undermine basic elements of our constitutional system and to manipulate the public through the withholding of information. For more than eight years, federal officials have had the authority to reclassify information already in the public domain and to restrict unclassified documents; regulatory agencies have bowed to the dictatorship of the Office of Management and Budget; valuable statistical programs have been cut back or eliminated entirely.

On many occasions, the Reagan and Bush administrations have counted on the short attention span of the public and the media. When objections were made to the policy of lifetime nondisclosure agreements, senior government officials announced plans to limit or rescind part of the policy, only to resume quietly the same course of action. The strategy has continued, and one of its more important consequences was that the fundamental issue of authority was never confronted. Dozens of executive orders and directives have been issued that may have no legal basis but have not been questioned because they carry the aura of presidential power.

While the clout of those in the White House has been increasing, lower-level government employees and those in academia and elsewhere whose livelihood depends on federal money have suffered particular erosion of their individual rights. Secrecy agreements, pre-publication review, polygraph testing, and drug testing are spreading as conditions of government employment and research contracts. Most people have no alternative but to comply with such requirements if they are to continue to practice their professions. A government job may largely define a person's ability to remain in a particular professional community—as with scientists employed in highly specialized fields, who can work only in a limited number of research institutions.

Secrecy restrictions are undermining scientific creativity as well as the free exchange of ideas in the academic world as researchers censor themselves for fear of violating federal regulations. The Reagan administration, preoccupied with preventing the release of sophisticated technical information to the Russians, created conditions under which there will be far fewer secrets to reveal.

In our time, the control of information is not just another issue; it is the central issue, and it largely determines the extent of public participation on other political and economic issues. Access to information has long been seen as the basis of an informed, aware population. Not so long ago, with the adoption of the Freedom of Information Act in 1966, access to information held by the federal government was established as a right.

In addition to direct assaults on access laws, the Reagan and Bush administrations have been working against the principle of an informed citizenry in their efforts to transfer essential information functions to the private sector. What is troubling about this policy is not the abstract question of ownership, but the fact that no steps have been taken to ensure that the public will continue to have access to important information—which, after all, was originally collected with taxpayer money.

The right of the public to have access to government information, including that which has been transferred to private hands, should be extended to the new channels for storing and transmitting information, with procedural guarantees and substantive definitions of the public's rights. This goal could be expressed in general terms that emphasize the public interest in access to the information resource. The analogy here is to the way that broadcast law established requirements that private television and radio licensees provide local information and program diversity in exchange for their right to use the public airwaves.

New Technology and the First Amendment

To many people, new information and communications technologies are the link between the problems of yesterday and the possibilities of tomorrow. They can open new channels, and broaden access to more types of information by millions of people.

In some ways, the technology dares us to confront the limits of our thinking. Satellites, for example, transmit across borders, transcending nation-states and national ideologies. Along with its great promise, this new form of information transmission is presenting new First Amendment issues.

In the past, regulations were issued to prevent companies from establishing a monopoly over local channels of communication; a firm could not own a newspaper and a radio station in the same town, for example. With satellites, the owner of a single satellite can transmit information throughout the continental United States, to Puerto Rico and the Caribbean, and, before long, to Western Europe and parts of Africa. The influence over hearts and minds augured by this capability is awesome.

So far, the concentration of control in this area has not received significant attention in the United States. This is not the case in nations less geographically isolated than the United States. What we have seen is the easing of traditional ownership limitations for broadcast stations, leading in the 1980s to a gold rush that has changed the contours of the electronic as well as the print media.

In contrast, some concerns about access have generated significant controversy about the future of free speech in the high-tech age. Not long ago, after images taken of the Soviet nuclear accident at Chernobyl were used in U.S. television newscasts, the networks announced their interest in owning a "remote sensing" satellite that could provide such images. The Pentagon, worried that this capability would allow the media to photograph military facilities, called the idea a threat to the "national security" and moved quickly to adopt regulations giving it the power to veto such plans. Now that news organizations are extending their capabilities through advanced technologies, how the public interest should be reconciled with the government's national security objectives remains to be resolved.

Computers also present important challenges to freedom of speech in America. The technology would seem to invite people to participate in or to create new channels of communication. But to use this technology requires money and skills that remain outside the reach of much of the population. The gulf between the computer fluent and nonfluent will become more serious as more and more information is available only through computerized databases and information services.

Librarians have argued that government policy should be

developed to address the ways that automated information systems will affect existing abilities to obtain information. Already libraries face the reality of having to cut back on acquisitions because of the rising costs of publications and overhead. Automated information systems pose even more daunting problems in keeping collections up to date.

The conversion of information to electronic form has also created difficulties with regard to access to government documents. Existing laws guarantee public access to government "records," a category that several federal agencies maintain does not include computerized information.

An example of one agency's attempt to deny access involves an FOIA request filed in 1987 at the Department of Energy by the National Security Archive in Washington, D.C. The Archive requested a list of unclassified reports stored in one of the Department of Energy's computerized databases. The department denied that the list existed and claimed that because the material was computerized, it was not required to assemble one. The Archive appealed, and an administrative judge ruled in its favor. While this decision was encouraging, it cannot be regarded as a solution to similar denials that may take place at dozens of other agencies. Stronger congressional guidance on the responsibilities of government agencies in the age of computers is long overdue.

Ahead stretches the landscape of the high-tech and a highly controlled society. If individual freedoms and pluralism are to be preserved, this must be accomplished through the combined efforts of policy makers, technology and information vendors, and consumers.

This is a next-stage problem. Today the United States faces the significant challenge of restoring the traditions of free speech and diversity of information that were eroded in the 1980s.

Index

190

193

ABOUT THE AUTHOR

Donna A. Demac is a lawyer, writer, and educator living in New York City. She teaches courses on copyright and domestic and international communications at New York University, and is the author of *Keeping America Uninformed: Government Secrecy in the 1980s*, and editor of *Tracing New Orbits: Cooperation and Competition in Global Satellite Development*. She has written widely on public access to information, and is on the board of the National Coalition Against Censorship.